Mometrix
TEST PREPARATION

CLEP®

Western Civilization I Exam Secrets Study Guide

CLEP® and College-Level Examination Program® are trademarks registered by the College Board, which is not affiliated with, and does not endorse, this product.

Dear Future Exam Success Story

First of all, **THANK YOU** for purchasing Mometrix study materials!

Second, congratulations! You are one of the few determined test-takers who are committed to doing whatever it takes to excel on your exam. **You have come to the right place.** We developed these study materials with one goal in mind: to deliver you the information you need in a format that's concise and easy to use.

In addition to optimizing your guide for the content of the test, we've outlined our recommended steps for breaking down the preparation process into small, attainable goals so you can make sure you stay on track.

We've also analyzed the entire test-taking process, identifying the most common pitfalls and showing how you can overcome them and be ready for any curveball the test throws you.

Standardized testing is one of the biggest obstacles on your road to success, which only increases the importance of doing well in the high-pressure, high-stakes environment of test day. Your results on this test could have a significant impact on your future, and this guide provides the information and practical advice to help you achieve your full potential on test day.

Your success is our success

We would love to hear from you! If you would like to share the story of your exam success or if you have any questions or comments in regard to our products, please contact us at **800-673-8175** or **support@mometrix.com**.

Thanks again for your business and we wish you continued success!

Sincerely,
The Mometrix Test Preparation Team

Need more help? Check out our flashcards at:
http://MometrixFlashcards.com/CLEP

Copyright © 2026 by Mometrix Media LLC. All rights reserved.
Written and edited by the Mometrix Exam Secrets Test Prep Team
Printed in the United States of America

Table of Contents

Introduction

Thank you for purchasing this resource! You have made the choice to prepare yourself for a test that could have a huge impact on your future, and this guide is designed to help you be fully ready for test day. Obviously, it's important to have a solid understanding of the test material, but you also need to be prepared for the unique environment and stressors of the test, so that you can perform to the best of your abilities.

For this purpose, the first section that appears in this guide is the **Secret Keys**. We've devoted countless hours to meticulously researching what works and what doesn't, and we've boiled down our findings to the five most impactful steps you can take to improve your performance on the test. We start at the beginning with study planning and move through the preparation process, all the way to the testing strategies that will help you get the most out of what you know when you're finally sitting in front of the test.

We recommend that you start preparing for your test as far in advance as possible. However, if you've bought this guide as a last-minute study resource and only have a few days before your test, we recommend that you skip over the first two Secret Keys since they address a long-term study plan.

If you struggle with **test anxiety**, we strongly encourage you to check out our recommendations for how you can overcome it. Test anxiety is a formidable foe, but it can be beaten, and we want to make sure you have the tools you need to defeat it.

Copyright © Mometrix Media. You have been licensed one copy of this document for personal use only. Any other reproduction or redistribution is strictly prohibited. All rights reserved.
This content is provided for test preparation purposes only and does not imply an endorsement by Mometrix of any particular political, scientific, or religious point of view.

Secret Key #1 – Plan Big, Study Small

There's a lot riding on your performance. If you want to ace this test, you're going to need to keep your skills sharp and the material fresh in your mind. You need a plan that lets you review everything you need to know while still fitting in your schedule. We'll break this strategy down into three categories.

Information Organization

Start with the information you already have: the official test outline. From this, you can make a complete list of all the concepts you need to cover before the test. Organize these concepts into groups that can be studied together, and create a list of any related vocabulary you need to learn so you can brush up on any difficult terms. You'll want to keep this vocabulary list handy once you actually start studying since you may need to add to it along the way.

Time Management

Once you have your set of study concepts, decide how to spread them out over the time you have left before the test. Break your study plan into small, clear goals so you have a manageable task for each day and know exactly what you're doing. Then just focus on one small step at a time. When you manage your time this way, you don't need to spend hours at a time studying. Studying a small block of content for a short period each day helps you retain information better and avoid stressing over how much you have left to do. You can relax knowing that you have a plan to cover everything in time. In order for this strategy to be effective though, you have to start studying early and stick to your schedule. Avoid the exhaustion and futility that comes from last-minute cramming!

Study Environment

The environment you study in has a big impact on your learning. Studying in a coffee shop, while probably more enjoyable, is not likely to be as fruitful as studying in a quiet room. It's important to keep distractions to a minimum. You're only planning to study for a short block of time, so make the most of it. Don't pause to check your phone or get up to find a snack. It's also important to **avoid multitasking**. Research has consistently shown that multitasking will make your studying dramatically less effective. Your study area should also be comfortable and well-lit so you don't have the distraction of straining your eyes or sitting on an uncomfortable chair.

The time of day you study is also important. You want to be rested and alert. Don't wait until just before bedtime. Study when you'll be most likely to comprehend and remember. Even better, if you know what time of day your test will be, set that time aside for study. That way your brain will be used to working on that subject at that specific time and you'll have a better chance of recalling information.

Finally, it can be helpful to team up with others who are studying for the same test. Your actual studying should be done in as isolated an environment as possible, but the work of organizing the information and setting up the study plan can be divided up. In between study sessions, you can discuss with your teammates the concepts that you're all studying and quiz each other on the details. Just be sure that your teammates are as serious about the test as you are. If you find that your study time is being replaced with social time, you might need to find a new team.

Copyright © Mometrix Media. You have been licensed one copy of this document for personal use only. Any other reproduction or redistribution is strictly prohibited. All rights reserved.
This content is provided for test preparation purposes only and does not imply an endorsement by Mometrix of any particular political, scientific, or religious point of view.

Secret Key #2 – Make Your Studying Count

You're devoting a lot of time and effort to preparing for this test, so you want to be absolutely certain it will pay off. This means doing more than just reading the content and hoping you can remember it on test day. It's important to make every minute of study count. There are two main areas you can focus on to make your studying count.

Retention

It doesn't matter how much time you study if you can't remember the material. You need to make sure you are retaining the concepts. To check your retention of the information you're learning, try recalling it at later times with minimal prompting. Try carrying around flashcards and glance at one or two from time to time or ask a friend who's also studying for the test to quiz you.

To enhance your retention, look for ways to put the information into practice so that you can apply it rather than simply recalling it. If you're using the information in practical ways, it will be much easier to remember. Similarly, it helps to solidify a concept in your mind if you're not only reading it to yourself but also explaining it to someone else. Ask a friend to let you teach them about a concept you're a little shaky on (or speak aloud to an imaginary audience if necessary). As you try to summarize, define, give examples, and answer your friend's questions, you'll understand the concepts better and they will stay with you longer. Finally, step back for a big picture view and ask yourself how each piece of information fits with the whole subject. When you link the different concepts together and see them working together as a whole, it's easier to remember the individual components.

Finally, practice showing your work on any multi-step problems, even if you're just studying. Writing out each step you take to solve a problem will help solidify the process in your mind, and you'll be more likely to remember it during the test.

Modality

Modality simply refers to the means or method by which you study. Choosing a study modality that fits your own individual learning style is crucial. No two people learn best in exactly the same way, so it's important to know your strengths and use them to your advantage.

For example, if you learn best by visualization, focus on visualizing a concept in your mind and draw an image or a diagram. Try color-coding your notes, illustrating them, or creating symbols that will trigger your mind to recall a learned concept. If you learn best by hearing or discussing information, find a study partner who learns the same way or read aloud to yourself. Think about how to put the information in your own words. Imagine that you are giving a lecture on the topic and record yourself so you can listen to it later.

For any learning style, flashcards can be helpful. Organize the information so you can take advantage of spare moments to review. Underline key words or phrases. Use different colors for different categories. Mnemonic devices (such as creating a short list in which every item starts with the same letter) can also help with retention. Find what works best for you and use it to store the information in your mind most effectively and easily.

Copyright © Mometrix Media. You have been licensed one copy of this document for personal use only. Any other reproduction or redistribution is strictly prohibited. All rights reserved.
This content is provided for test preparation purposes only and does not imply an endorsement by Mometrix of any particular political, scientific, or religious point of view.

Secret Key #3 – Practice the Right Way

Your success on test day depends not only on how many hours you put into preparing, but also on whether you prepared the right way. It's good to check along the way to see if your studying is paying off. One of the most effective ways to do this is by taking practice tests to evaluate your progress. Practice tests are useful because they show exactly where you need to improve. Every time you take a practice test, pay special attention to these three groups of questions:

- The questions you got wrong
- The questions you had to guess on, even if you guessed right
- The questions you found difficult or slow to work through

This will show you exactly what your weak areas are, and where you need to devote more study time. Ask yourself why each of these questions gave you trouble. Was it because you didn't understand the material? Was it because you didn't remember the vocabulary? Do you need more repetitions on this type of question to build speed and confidence? Dig into those questions and figure out how you can strengthen your weak areas as you go back to review the material.

Additionally, many practice tests have a section explaining the answer choices. It can be tempting to read the explanation and think that you now have a good understanding of the concept. However, an explanation likely only covers part of the question's broader context. Even if the explanation makes perfect sense, **go back and investigate** every concept related to the question until you're positive you have a thorough understanding.

As you go along, keep in mind that the practice test is just that: practice. Memorizing these questions and answers will not be very helpful on the actual test because it is unlikely to have any of the same exact questions. If you only know the right answers to the sample questions, you won't be prepared for the real thing. **Study the concepts** until you understand them fully, and then you'll be able to answer any question that shows up on the test.

It's important to wait on the practice tests until you're ready. If you take a test on your first day of study, you may be overwhelmed by the amount of material covered and how much you need to learn. Work up to it gradually.

On test day, you'll need to be prepared for answering questions, managing your time, and using the test-taking strategies you've learned. It's a lot to balance, like a mental marathon that will have a big impact on your future. Like training for a marathon, you'll need to start slowly and work your way up. When test day arrives, you'll be ready.

Start with the strategies you've read in the first two Secret Keys—plan your course and study in the way that works best for you. If you have time, consider using multiple study resources to get different approaches to the same concepts. It can be helpful to see difficult concepts from more than one angle. Then find a good source for practice tests. Many times, the test website will suggest potential study resources or provide sample tests.

Copyright © Mometrix Media. You have been licensed one copy of this document for personal use only. Any other reproduction or redistribution is strictly prohibited. All rights reserved.
This content is provided for test preparation purposes only and does not imply an endorsement by Mometrix of any particular political, scientific, or religious point of view.

Practice Test Strategy

If you're able to find at least three practice tests, we recommend this strategy:

UNTIMED AND OPEN-BOOK PRACTICE

Take the first test with no time constraints and with your notes and study guide handy. Take your time and focus on applying the strategies you've learned.

TIMED AND OPEN-BOOK PRACTICE

Take the second practice test open-book as well, but set a timer and practice pacing yourself to finish in time.

TIMED AND CLOSED-BOOK PRACTICE

Take any other practice tests as if it were test day. Set a timer and put away your study materials. Sit at a table or desk in a quiet room, imagine yourself at the testing center, and answer questions as quickly and accurately as possible.

Keep repeating timed and closed-book tests on a regular basis until you run out of practice tests or it's time for the actual test. Your mind will be ready for the schedule and stress of test day, and you'll be able to focus on recalling the material you've learned.

Copyright © Mometrix Media. You have been licensed one copy of this document for personal use only. Any other reproduction or redistribution is strictly prohibited. All rights reserved.
This content is provided for test preparation purposes only and does not imply an endorsement by Mometrix of any particular political, scientific, or religious point of view.

Secret Key #4 – Pace Yourself

Once you're fully prepared for the material on the test, your biggest challenge on test day will be managing your time. Just knowing that the clock is ticking can make you panic even if you have plenty of time left. Work on pacing yourself so you can build confidence against the time constraints of the exam. Pacing is a difficult skill to master, especially in a high-pressure environment, so **practice is vital**.

Set time expectations for your pace based on how much time is available. For example, if a section has 60 questions and the time limit is 30 minutes, you know you have to average 30 seconds or less per question in order to answer them all. Although 30 seconds is the hard limit, set 25 seconds per question as your goal, so you reserve extra time to spend on harder questions. When you budget extra time for the harder questions, you no longer have any reason to stress when those questions take longer to answer.

Don't let this time expectation distract you from working through the test at a calm, steady pace, but keep it in mind so you don't spend too much time on any one question. Recognize that taking extra time on one question you don't understand may keep you from answering two that you do understand later in the test. If your time limit for a question is up and you're still not sure of the answer, mark it and move on, and come back to it later if the time and the test format allow. If the testing format doesn't allow you to return to earlier questions, just make an educated guess; then put it out of your mind and move on.

On the easier questions, be careful not to rush. It may seem wise to hurry through them so you have more time for the challenging ones, but it's not worth missing one if you know the concept and just didn't take the time to read the question fully. Work efficiently but make sure you understand the question and have looked at all of the answer choices, since more than one may seem right at first.

Even if you're paying attention to the time, you may find yourself a little behind at some point. You should speed up to get back on track, but do so wisely. Don't panic; just take a few seconds less on each question until you're caught up. Don't guess without thinking, but do look through the answer choices and eliminate any you know are wrong. If you can get down to two choices, it is often worthwhile to guess from those. Once you've chosen an answer, move on and don't dwell on any that you skipped or had to hurry through. If a question was taking too long, chances are it was one of the harder ones, so you weren't as likely to get it right anyway.

On the other hand, if you find yourself getting ahead of schedule, it may be beneficial to slow down a little. The more quickly you work, the more likely you are to make a careless mistake that will affect your score. You've budgeted time for each question, so don't be afraid to spend that time. Practice an efficient but careful pace to get the most out of the time you have.

Copyright © Mometrix Media. You have been licensed one copy of this document for personal use only. Any other reproduction or redistribution is strictly prohibited. All rights reserved.
This content is provided for test preparation purposes only and does not imply an endorsement by Mometrix of any particular political, scientific, or religious point of view.

Secret Key #5 – Have a Plan for Guessing

When you're taking the test, you may find yourself stuck on a question. Some of the answer choices seem better than others, but you don't see the one answer choice that is obviously correct. What do you do?

The scenario described above is very common, yet most test takers have not effectively prepared for it. Developing and practicing a plan for guessing may be one of the single most effective uses of your time as you get ready for the exam.

In developing your plan for guessing, there are three questions to address:

- When should you start the guessing process?
- How should you narrow down the choices?
- Which answer should you choose?

When to Start the Guessing Process

Unless your plan for guessing is to select C every time (which, despite its merits, is not what we recommend), you need to leave yourself enough time to apply your answer elimination strategies. Since you have a limited amount of time for each question, that means that if you're going to give yourself the best shot at guessing correctly, you have to decide quickly whether or not you will guess.

Of course, the best-case scenario is that you don't have to guess at all, so first, see if you can answer the question based on your knowledge of the subject and basic reasoning skills. Focus on the key words in the question and try to jog your memory of related topics. Give yourself a chance to bring the knowledge to mind, but once you realize that you don't have (or you can't access) the knowledge you need to answer the question, it's time to start the guessing process.

It's almost always better to start the guessing process too early than too late. It only takes a few seconds to remember something and answer the question from knowledge. Carefully eliminating wrong answer choices takes longer. Plus, going through the process of eliminating answer choices can actually help jog your memory.

Summary: Start the guessing process as soon as you decide that you can't answer the question based on your knowledge.

Copyright © Mometrix Media. You have been licensed one copy of this document for personal use only. Any other reproduction or redistribution is strictly prohibited. All rights reserved.
This content is provided for test preparation purposes only and does not imply an endorsement by Mometrix of any particular political, scientific, or religious point of view.

How to Narrow Down the Choices

The next chapter in this book (**Test-Taking Strategies**) includes a wide range of strategies for how to approach questions and how to look for answer choices to eliminate. You will definitely want to read those carefully, practice them, and figure out which ones work best for you. Here though, we're going to address a mindset rather than a particular strategy.

Your odds of guessing an answer correctly depend on how many options you are choosing from.

Number of options left	5	4	3	2	1
Odds of guessing correctly	20%	25%	33%	50%	100%

You can see from this chart just how valuable it is to be able to eliminate incorrect answers and make an educated guess, but there are two things that many test takers do that cause them to miss out on the benefits of guessing:

- Accidentally eliminating the correct answer
- Selecting an answer based on an impression

We'll look at the first one here, and the second one in the next section.

To avoid accidentally eliminating the correct answer, we recommend a thought exercise called **the $5 challenge**. In this challenge, you only eliminate an answer choice from contention if you are willing to bet $5 on it being wrong. Why $5? Five dollars is a small but not insignificant amount of money. It's an amount you could afford to lose but wouldn't want to throw away. And while losing $5 once might not hurt too much, doing it twenty times will set you back $100. In the same way, each small decision you make—eliminating a choice here, guessing on a question there—won't by itself impact your score very much, but when you put them all together, they can make a big difference. By holding each answer choice elimination decision to a higher standard, you can reduce the risk of accidentally eliminating the correct answer.

The $5 challenge can also be applied in a positive sense: If you are willing to bet $5 that an answer choice *is* correct, go ahead and mark it as correct.

Summary: Only eliminate an answer choice if you are willing to bet $5 that it is wrong.

Copyright © Mometrix Media. You have been licensed one copy of this document for personal use only. Any other reproduction or redistribution is strictly prohibited. All rights reserved.
This content is provided for test preparation purposes only and does not imply an endorsement by Mometrix of any particular political, scientific, or religious point of view.

Which Answer to Choose

You're taking the test. You've run into a hard question and decided you'll have to guess. You've eliminated all the answer choices you're willing to bet $5 on. Now you have to pick an answer. Why do we even need to talk about this? Why can't you just pick whichever one you feel like when the time comes?

The answer to these questions is that if you don't come into the test with a plan, you'll rely on your impression to select an answer choice, and if you do that, you risk falling into a trap. The test writers know that everyone who takes their test will be guessing on some of the questions, so they intentionally write wrong answer choices to seem plausible. You still have to pick an answer though, and if the wrong answer choices are designed to look right, how can you ever be sure that you're not falling for their trap? The best solution we've found to this dilemma is to take the decision out of your hands entirely. Here is the process we recommend:

Once you've eliminated any choices that you are confident (willing to bet $5) are wrong, select the first remaining choice as your answer.

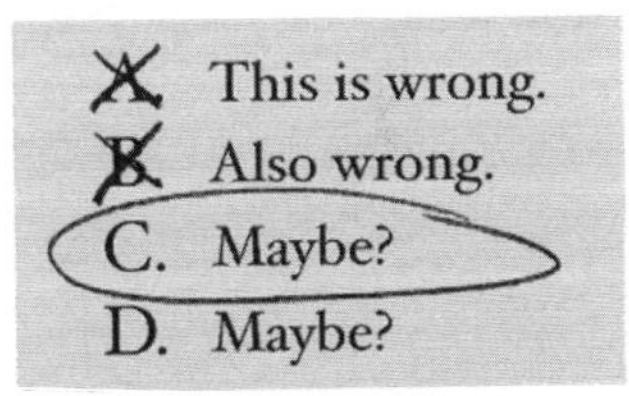

Whether you choose to select the first remaining choice, the second, or the last, the important thing is that you use some preselected standard. Using this approach guarantees that you will not be enticed into selecting an answer choice that looks right, because you are not basing your decision on how the answer choices look.

This is not meant to make you question your knowledge. Instead, it is to help you recognize the difference between your knowledge and your impressions. There's a huge difference between thinking an answer is right because of what you know, and thinking an answer is right because it looks or sounds like it should be right.

Summary: To ensure that your selection is appropriately random, make a predetermined selection from among all answer choices you have not eliminated.

Copyright © Mometrix Media. You have been licensed one copy of this document for personal use only. Any other reproduction or redistribution is strictly prohibited. All rights reserved.
This content is provided for test preparation purposes only and does not imply an endorsement by Mometrix of any particular political, scientific, or religious point of view.

Test-Taking Strategies

This section contains a list of test-taking strategies that you may find helpful as you work through the test. By taking what you know and applying logical thought, you can maximize your chances of answering any question correctly!

It is very important to realize that every question is different and every person is different: no single strategy will work on every question, and no single strategy will work for every person. That's why we've included all of them here, so you can try them out and determine which ones work best for different types of questions and which ones work best for you.

Question Strategies

☑ Read Carefully

Read the question and the answer choices carefully. Don't miss the question because you misread the terms. You have plenty of time to read each question thoroughly and make sure you understand what is being asked. Yet a happy medium must be attained, so don't waste too much time. You must read carefully and efficiently.

☑ Contextual Clues

Look for contextual clues. If the question includes a word you are not familiar with, look at the immediate context for some indication of what the word might mean. Contextual clues can often give you all the information you need to decipher the meaning of an unfamiliar word. Even if you can't determine the meaning, you may be able to narrow down the possibilities enough to make a solid guess at the answer to the question.

☑ Prefixes

If you're having trouble with a word in the question or answer choices, try dissecting it. Take advantage of every clue that the word might include. Prefixes can be a huge help. Usually, they allow you to determine a basic meaning. *Pre-* means before, *post-* means after, *pro-* is positive, *de-* is negative. From prefixes, you can get an idea of the general meaning of the word and try to put it into context.

☑ Hedge Words

Watch out for critical hedge words, such as *likely, may, can, often, almost, mostly, usually, generally, rarely*, and *sometimes*. Question writers insert these hedge phrases to cover every possibility. Often an answer choice will be wrong simply because it leaves no room for exception. Be on guard for answer choices that have definitive words such as *exactly* and *always*.

☑ Switchback Words

Stay alert for *switchbacks*. These are the words and phrases frequently used to alert you to shifts in thought. The most common switchback words are *but, although*, and *however*. Others include *nevertheless, on the other hand, even though, while, in spite of, despite*, and *regardless of*. Switchback words are important to catch because they can change the direction of the question or an answer choice.

Copyright © Mometrix Media. You have been licensed one copy of this document for personal use only. Any other reproduction or redistribution is strictly prohibited. All rights reserved.
This content is provided for test preparation purposes only and does not imply an endorsement by Mometrix of any particular political, scientific, or religious point of view.

⊘ Face Value

When in doubt, use common sense. Accept the situation in the problem at face value. Don't read too much into it. These problems will not require you to make wild assumptions. If you have to go beyond creativity and warp time or space in order to have an answer choice fit the question, then you should move on and consider the other answer choices. These are normal problems rooted in reality. The applicable relationship or explanation may not be readily apparent, but it is there for you to figure out. Use your common sense to interpret anything that isn't clear.

Answer Choice Strategies

⊘ Answer Selection

The most thorough way to pick an answer choice is to identify and eliminate wrong answers until only one is left, then confirm it is the correct answer. Sometimes an answer choice may immediately seem right, but be careful. The test writers will usually put more than one reasonable answer choice on each question, so take a second to read all of them and make sure that the other choices are not equally obvious. As long as you have time left, it is better to read every answer choice than to pick the first one that looks right without checking the others.

⊘ Answer Choice Families

An answer choice family consists of two (in rare cases, three) answer choices that are very similar in construction and cannot all be true at the same time. If you see two answer choices that are direct opposites or parallels, one of them is usually the correct answer. For instance, if one answer choice says that quantity *x* increases and another either says that quantity *x* decreases (opposite) or says that quantity *y* increases (parallel), then those answer choices would fall into the same family. An answer choice that doesn't match the construction of the answer choice family is more likely to be incorrect. Most questions will not have answer choice families, but when they do appear, you should be prepared to recognize them.

⊘ Eliminate Answers

Eliminate answer choices as soon as you realize they are wrong, but make sure you consider all possibilities. If you are eliminating answer choices and realize that the last one you are left with is also wrong, don't panic. Start over and consider each choice again. There may be something you missed the first time that you will realize on the second pass.

⊘ Avoid Fact Traps

Don't be distracted by an answer choice that is factually true but doesn't answer the question. You are looking for the choice that answers the question. Stay focused on what the question is asking for so you don't accidentally pick an answer that is true but incorrect. Always go back to the question and make sure the answer choice you've selected actually answers the question and is not merely a true statement.

⊘ Extreme Statements

In general, you should avoid answers that put forth extreme actions as standard practice or proclaim controversial ideas as established fact. An answer choice that states the "process should be used in certain situations, if..." is much more likely to be correct than one that states the "process should be discontinued completely." The first is a calm rational statement and doesn't even make a definitive, uncompromising stance, using a hedge word *if* to provide wiggle room, whereas the second choice is far more extreme.

Copyright © Mometrix Media. You have been licensed one copy of this document for personal use only. Any other reproduction or redistribution is strictly prohibited. All rights reserved.
This content is provided for test preparation purposes only and does not imply an endorsement by Mometrix of any particular political, scientific, or religious point of view.

⊘ BENCHMARK

As you read through the answer choices and you come across one that seems to answer the question well, mentally select that answer choice. This is not your final answer, but it's the one that will help you evaluate the other answer choices. The one that you selected is your benchmark or standard for judging each of the other answer choices. Every other answer choice must be compared to your benchmark. That choice is correct until proven otherwise by another answer choice beating it. If you find a better answer, then that one becomes your new benchmark. Once you've decided that no other choice answers the question as well as your benchmark, you have your final answer.

⊘ PREDICT THE ANSWER

Before you even start looking at the answer choices, it is often best to try to predict the answer. When you come up with the answer on your own, it is easier to avoid distractions and traps because you will know exactly what to look for. The right answer choice is unlikely to be word-for-word what you came up with, but it should be a close match. Even if you are confident that you have the right answer, you should still take the time to read each option before moving on.

General Strategies

⊘ TOUGH QUESTIONS

If you are stumped on a problem or it appears too hard or too difficult, don't waste time. Move on! Remember though, if you can quickly check for obviously incorrect answer choices, your chances of guessing correctly are greatly improved. Before you completely give up, at least try to knock out a couple of possible answers. Eliminate what you can and then guess at the remaining answer choices before moving on.

⊘ CHECK YOUR WORK

Since you will probably not know every term listed and the answer to every question, it is important that you get credit for the ones that you do know. Don't miss any questions through careless mistakes. If at all possible, try to take a second to look back over your answer selection and make sure you've selected the correct answer choice and haven't made a costly careless mistake (such as marking an answer choice that you didn't mean to mark). This quick double check should more than pay for itself in caught mistakes for the time it costs.

⊘ PACE YOURSELF

It's easy to be overwhelmed when you're looking at a page full of questions; your mind is confused and full of random thoughts, and the clock is ticking down faster than you would like. Calm down and maintain the pace that you have set for yourself. Especially as you get down to the last few minutes of the test, don't let the small numbers on the clock make you panic. As long as you are on track by monitoring your pace, you are guaranteed to have time for each question.

⊘ DON'T RUSH

It is very easy to make errors when you are in a hurry. Maintaining a fast pace in answering questions is pointless if it makes you miss questions that you would have gotten right otherwise. Test writers like to include distracting information and wrong answers that seem right. Taking a little extra time to avoid careless mistakes can make all the difference in your test score. Find a pace that allows you to be confident in the answers that you select.

Copyright © Mometrix Media. You have been licensed one copy of this document for personal use only. Any other reproduction or redistribution is strictly prohibited. All rights reserved.
This content is provided for test preparation purposes only and does not imply an endorsement by Mometrix of any particular political, scientific, or religious point of view.

⊘ Keep Moving

Panicking will not help you pass the test, so do your best to stay calm and keep moving. Taking deep breaths and going through the answer elimination steps you practiced can help to break through a stress barrier and keep your pace.

Final Notes

The combination of a solid foundation of content knowledge and the confidence that comes from practicing your plan for applying that knowledge is the key to maximizing your performance on test day. As your foundation of content knowledge is built up and strengthened, you'll find that the strategies included in this chapter become more and more effective in helping you quickly sift through the distractions and traps of the test to isolate the correct answer.

Now that you're preparing to move forward into the test content chapters of this book, be sure to keep your goal in mind. As you read, think about how you will be able to apply this information on the test. If you've already seen sample questions for the test and you have an idea of the question format and style, try to come up with questions of your own that you can answer based on what you're reading. This will give you valuable practice applying your knowledge in the same ways you can expect to on test day.

Good luck and good studying!

Copyright © Mometrix Media. You have been licensed one copy of this document for personal use only. Any other reproduction or redistribution is strictly prohibited. All rights reserved.
This content is provided for test preparation purposes only and does not imply an endorsement by Mometrix of any particular political, scientific, or religious point of view.

Copyright © Mometrix Media. You have been licensed one copy of this document for personal use only. Any other reproduction or redistribution is strictly prohibited. All rights reserved.
This content is provided for test preparation purposes only and does not imply an endorsement by Mometrix of any particular political, scientific, or religious point of view.

Ancient Greece and Hellenistic Civilization

Facts about the Minoan civilization

- Arose around 2000 B.C, on the island of Crete
- Capital at Knossos
- Named after King Minos
- Minos built a great palace in Knossos. Its walls were covered in frescoes, paintings made on wet plaster.
- Artists created elaborate seals and pottery
- Art often depicted animal figures like bulls
- Cities had paved streets and piped water systems
- Society was matriarchal
- Used forms of writing now called Linear A and Linear B
- Established extensive trade networks
- Were skilled sailors and traders with outposts throughout the Aegean Sea and Asia Minor and had a strong navy to protect trading ships
- Volcanic eruption on Thera c. 1500 caused earthquakes that destroyed much of Knossos
- Conquered by the Mycenaeans, c. 1450 B.C.

Mycenaeans

The Mycenaeans were a warrior culture with several levels of political and social organization. Family ties were apparently very important to this structure. Several related families made up a clan with each clan headed by a strong warrior. Several clans made up a tribe, headed by a chief, or king. The chief appointed several officials, including the commander of the army. The Myceneans built strong, fort-like towns, led by Mycenae, from which the group takes its name. They worshipped gods of war and blood, represented by the sky, thunder, and mountains. Scholars believe the Mycenean language formed the basis for ancient Greek. The Mycenean culture was weakened by fighting between clans and tribes. They were conquered by another invading group, possibly the Dorians, though scholars debate the true origins of the legendary Dorians.

Development of the city-state in ancient Greece

Possibly following the example of the Mycenaeans, most Greek tribes built forts high on hills for protection. As the populations around these forts grew, the concept of the polis, or city-state, emerged. The city-states came to include the fort with its surrounding city, farmlands and nearby farming villages. Unlike previous forms of organization, city-states were based more on geographic proximity than ethnic or familial ties. Every resident of the city-state contributed to the good of the whole and received benefits in kind. The fort and its soldiers protected the central city and the villages. In turn, the residents worked together in various jobs to maintain order. The farmlands and villages protected by the fort and the government provided food for the population. The city-states acted independently of one another. Over time, city-states developed strong identities. The citizens were extremely proud of, and loyal to, their city-states. Eventually, however, this pride led to rivalries between some city-states.

Copyright © Mometrix Media. You have been licensed one copy of this document for personal use only. Any other reproduction or redistribution is strictly prohibited. All rights reserved.
This content is provided for test preparation purposes only and does not imply an endorsement by Mometrix of any particular political, scientific, or religious point of view.

Birthplace of Democracy

Some Greek city-states, especially Athens, developed the practice of allowing citizens to take part in government. The Athenians came to call this idea *demokratia,* or "democracy," from the words *demos,* meaning "people," and *kratos,* meaning "rule." The idea began to emerge after 650 B.C., during a period when many city-states overthrew their tyrant leaders. Some aristocratic leaders, especially in Athens, began to embrace the concept of popular government. Some practiced direct democracy, in which the voting citizens had to approve any laws or decisions by the government. Still, Greek democracy was very limited compared to modern democracy. Free women and slaves, who made up a large majority of the Athenian population, had no political rights. In some city-states only native-born, wealthy or landowning males could vote.

Ancient Greek Politics

Aristocrats — wealthy nobles who controlled political, economic, and military life in the early city-states; the term *aristocracy* meant "rule by the best"; aristocrats were the only citizens to take part in government, make laws, or act as judges; they also influenced religion, as it was widely believed that the gods spoke only to members of the aristocracy; in early Athens, the aristocratic class was known as the eupatrid

Hoplites — foot soldiers who served as primary guardians of the city-states; benefited from the economic success of the non-aristocratic middle class, who helped pay for their weapons, thus breaking the monopoly of the aristocracy; due to their increased defensive role, the hoplites demanded a greater role in government

Tyrants — individuals who seized absolute power in the city-states; they initially succeeded because the public believed they would rule better than the nobles; some did, but others turned into harsh dictators who used their military power to impose their will on the public, thus leading to the modern word *tyrant* meaning an unjust ruler

Sparta

Social and Political Structure of Sparta

Sparta was formed when northern invaders overran the Peloponnesus region of Messenia in the 1100s B.C. Its social and political structure contained three levels:

- Equals — highest level; full citizens descended from the northern invaders; controlled the land and government, organized as such:
- Two kings — one for military affairs, one for domestic affairs
- Council of Elders — 28 males over the age of 60; made laws and led criminal court
- Assembly — legislative body which voted on laws proposed by the Council of Elders; included all male citizens over age 30
- Ephorate — Five men elected each year by the assembly to oversee actions of government; could veto decisions by kings, council, or assembly
- Perioeci — half-citizens; free peoples who earned wages through skilled work; paid taxes, but could not serve in government leadership
- Helots — enslaved peoples; most descended from original Messenians; formed the majority of the population and performed most of the work, but had no political rights or freedoms

Copyright © Mometrix Media. You have been licensed one copy of this document for personal use only. Any other reproduction or redistribution is strictly prohibited. All rights reserved.
This content is provided for test preparation purposes only and does not imply an endorsement by Mometrix of any particular political, scientific, or religious point of view.

Athens

Social and Political Structure of Ancient Athens

Athens evolved as a seaport trade city, influenced by constant interaction with other peoples. Its social and political structure contained three levels:

- Citizens — Athenian-born men; had full political rights; could own land; paid taxes; might be wealthy or poor. Served in government, organized as such:
- Archons — nine officials who served one-year terms, split duties once held by king; had to be landowning citizens; members included:
- Archon proper — Main officer over civil and judicial issues, presided over archon council and Ecclesia
- Polemarch — Commander of army during war; also served as judge over foreigners
- Basileus — Primary religious leader
- Ecclesia — Assembly made up of all citizens; elected archons, generals and any other leaders
- Metics — Foreign-born, non-citizen residents; free people who earned wages through skilled work and paid same tax rate as citizens; unable to own land or serve in government; majority of the population
- Slaves — Mainly prisoners of war or debtors; most owned by individual citizens; some purchased freedom to became metics

Contributions to the Political Developments of Ancient Athens

- Draco — Archon who created Athens' first written code of laws around 621 B.C.; imposed death penalty for most infractions, giving rise to term "draconian"
- Solon — Archon who headed off potential class war around 600 B.C. by forgiving individual debts, freeing indebted slaves, and outlawing enslavement for debts; established four-tiered system of citizenship based on wealth; only members of wealthiest two tiers could hold office
- Peisistratus — Tyrant who ruled from 546 B.C. to 527 B.C.; policies united Athens, increased city-state pride; improved public works, economy, and diplomatic ties; after his death, citizens regained their role in government, but continued policies of Peisistratus
- Cleisthenes — Considered founder of Athenian democracy; archon who seized power around 508 B.C. with public support, then created system of direct democracy; divided citizenry into 10 tribes; each tribe elected 50 representatives to serve on Council of 500, a legislative body which proposed laws that were voted on by all citizens

Persian Wars

By 500 B.C., Persia was becoming a dominant force in the ancient world, mainly by controlling trade. Several Greek city-states in Asia Minor rebelled against Persian domination. Athens lent its support to the city-states. Persia, led by Darius, easily defeated the rebellion, but used Athens's support to justify invasion of the Greek mainland. This effort led to a series of conflicts collectively called the Persian Wars.

In 492 B.C., Persian forces conquered Thrace and Macedonia. In 490 B.C., they invaded mainland Greece, but were repelled in the Battle of Marathon. In 480 B.C., the Persians attacked again, but were met by a united force of troops from various city-states, including Sparta. At Thermopylae, 300 Spartans fought to the death, allowing Greek forces time to regroup. The Persians sacked Athens, but the Persian navy was defeated by the smaller, more maneuverable Greek ships in the

Copyright © Mometrix Media. You have been licensed one copy of this document for personal use only. Any other reproduction or redistribution is strictly prohibited. All rights reserved.
This content is provided for test preparation purposes only and does not imply an endorsement by Mometrix of any particular political, scientific, or religious point of view.

Salamis Strait. In 479 B.C., a combined army of Spartans and Athenians defeated the Persians at Plataea, effectively ending the Persian threat.

Delian League

After the Persian Wars, leaders of the Greek city-states came to believe they needed greater unity in order to protect themselves from outside invaders. Athenian leaders pressed for a formal alliance for mutual protection. They formed the *Delian League* as an alliance of 140 city-states. Representatives of the member city-states were supposed to meet annually, with each city-state having one vote. Member city-states contributed money and ships for mutual protection. Funds were initially kept on the island of Delos, from which the name of the league arose, but were later moved to Athens, whose leaders managed the funds. Through control of the Delian League, Athens expanded its influence over all of the city-states. Ultimately this power increased resentment against Athens.

Age of Pericles

Period named for Athenian leader, Pericles, who served in various offices from 461 B.C. to 429 B.C. Under his leadership, Athens came to dominate Greek culture. Major accomplishments included:

- expanded democracy so that all but the lowest level of citizens could hold public office
- officeholders received salaries
- officeholders chosen by lottery
- Athenians established colonies in key outposts
- Athenian navy expanded
- Athenian standard of weights and measure widely adopted
- Delian League treasury transferred from Delos to Athens
- Athens came to totally dominate Delian League
- some city-states began to rebel against Athenian dominance

Role of Trade in the Ancient Athenian Economy

Because of Athens's location as a port city, as well as its poor soil, its economy was dominated by trade. Athenian farmers had trouble growing the types of food crops needed to support large-scale populations. Using the terracing method, they were able to grow figs, olives, and grapes on hillsides. These crops, alone or processed into oil or wine, proved very popular as trade goods. The Athenians exported most of their crops and imported food staples and other items they could not obtain on their own. Eventually, Athens developed colonies spread throughout the region to aid its trade economy and provide resources they were not able to obtain at home.

Peloponnesian Wars

Causes —

- The rise of Athenian power under Pericles fostered widespread resentment among other city-states, especially independent-minded Sparta.
- Some city-states formed an alliance with Sparta to challenge Athens.
- Sparta had a stronger army, but Athens had a stronger navy. In 431 B.C., the Spartans invaded Attica, a peninsula outside of Athens, sparking the Peloponnesian Wars.

Effects —

- Despite a few victories, Athens weakened as the conflict dragged on.
- Sparta sought aid from the Persians.

Copyright © Mometrix Media. You have been licensed one copy of this document for personal use only. Any other reproduction or redistribution is strictly prohibited. All rights reserved.
This content is provided for test preparation purposes only and does not imply an endorsement by Mometrix of any particular political, scientific, or religious point of view.

- Athens's navy was destroyed by combined Spartan/Persian forces in 405 B.C.
- Athens finally surrendered in 404 B.C. after its enemies blocked Athenian food supplies.
- After the fall of Athens, the city-states struggled with one another for dominance. Sparta, the great military power, proved ineffective at political leadership across a large region.
- Some Greeks came to believe that only foreign, non-Greek leadership could unify and stabilize the region.

The Iliad and The Odyssey

Both are epic poems written in the 700s B.C. and credited to a blind poet named Homer, though the identity of the real author or authors is uncertain. The poems survived in oral form throughout the ages and reveal much about ancient Greek culture and history. They are considered among the greatest literary works of ancient western civilization. Both poems involve the Trojan War, one of the many conflicts between city-states. According to the *Iliad,* the war began when the Trojan prince Paris kidnapped the beautiful Helen, wife of Mycenaean king Agamemnon. The Mycenaeans lay siege to Troy for 10 years, attempting to get Helen back. They finally defeated Troy with the Trojan Horse, a giant wooden sculpture presented to the city as a gift, but which really housed Mycenaean troops. The *Odyssey* tells the story of the Ithacan Odysseus, as he tries to make his way back home following the Trojan War. His journey takes ten years, as he is distracted by various adventures, many involving gods and creatures from Greek mythology.

Major gods and goddesses of ancient Greek religion

- Zeus — King of all gods; reigns on Mount Olympus in northern Greece; father of many of the lesser gods, with various goddesses as well as mortal women
- Poseidon — brother of Zeus; god of the sea and water
- Hera — wife of Zeus; goddess of marriage and family
- Hades — god of the underworld
- Athena —goddess of wisdom, war, handicrafts, and reason; protector of cities; sprang from Zeus's head
- Artemis — goddess of Olympus; twin of Apollo
- Apollo — "most Greek of all the gods;" god of light, truth, music, and poetry
- Hermes —messenger god; god of commerce and trade
- Dionysus — god of fertility and wine
- Aphrodite — goddess of love and beauty
- Ares — god of war
- Haphaestus — craftsman god
- Demeter — goddess of corn
- Hestia — goddess of the hearth

Role of mythology in Greek culture

Myths helped the Greeks explain mysteries of the universe and served a central role in Greek religion and culture. The Greek religion placed very little emphasis on moral behavior or the afterlife. Greeks were mainly concerned with maintaining order and understanding the mysteries of the universe. Myths, or stories about the gods and goddesses, helped Greeks understand the mysteries such as how nature worked, how human emotions led to loss of self-control, and how Greeks could improve their own life on Earth. The myths revealed the lessons of the gods. Some explained how parts of the natural world came to be, while others involved flawed heroes who set out on a task or challenge through which the listener could learn lessons.

Copyright © Mometrix Media. You have been licensed one copy of this document for personal use only. Any other reproduction or redistribution is strictly prohibited. All rights reserved.
This content is provided for test preparation purposes only and does not imply an endorsement by Mometrix of any particular political, scientific, or religious point of view.

ROLES OF WOMEN IN ANCIENT ATHENIAN SOCIETY

Generally, Greek women were considered inferior to men. Because boys were preferred over girls, infanticide and abandonment of females was common among poorer families. Women were expected to remain separate and hidden from the realm of men. Females' main tasks were to manage the household, including servants, and raise the youngest children. However, the rights of women varied among city-states. Athenian-born women, for example, were considered citizens, but they were not allowed to vote, own or inherit property, or serve in any government office. In contrast, Spartan women were allowed to own and inherit property, and were considered outspoken compared to other city-states. In Athens, girls received no formal education and were usually wed, in marriages arranged by their parents, upon reaching puberty. Spartan women usually waited until age 18 to wed. Before that, they received some education and participated in many of the same athletic competitions as boys.

ATHENIAN EDUCATIONAL SYSTEM

PEDAGOGUES AND SOPHISTS

At the age of six, wealthy Athenian boys left the care of their mothers to be educated and trained by pedagogues, who were male slaves. The pedagogues taught the boys manners and, when the boys were ready to attend group classes, accompanied them to school and oversaw their progress. In essence, the pedagogues took over responsibility for raising the boys.

The Sophists were traveling educators and lecturers whose name derived from the Greek word meaning "wise." In the 400s B.C., one group of Sophists developed a school for older Athenian boys which emphasized different skills from the lower age levels in order to better prepare young men for leadership.

LEVELS OF EDUCATION FOR WEALTHY ATHENIAN MALES

There were three main levels of education for wealthy Athenian males:

- Younger boys, above age six or seven, attended group schools, similar to modern elementary schools, in which they learned reading, writing, poetry, grammar, music, and gymnastics. Physical fitness was an integral part of their education, reflecting the Greek belief in a strong mind-body connection. The boys participated in many field sports, such as running, jumping, boxing, discus throwing, and javelin throwing.
- After the creation of the Sophists' school, teenage boys began their preparation for leadership by focusing their studies on government, mathematics, ethics, and rhetoric.
- At age 18, every male citizen began a term of military service that lasted at least one year. Since soldiers provided much of their own equipment, their duties usually reflected their wealth. Those who could afford the best armor and weapons fought in the center of the phalanxes.

OLYMPIC GAMES

The Greeks considered physical strength and skills to be very important. They also took great pride in their allegiance to their city-states. Some city-states began to incorporate athletic competitions into their religious festivals, which soon grew into competitions between athletes from different city-states. The Olympic Games, so-called because there were held at Olympia to honor Zeus, emerged as the most enduring of these contests. The first recorded Olympics occurred in 776 B.C. and only included foot races. The games proved so popular they were held every four years until the Romans outlawed them in A.D. 400. The contests came to include many sports, including a variety of foot races, long jump, javelin discus throws, boxing, wrestling, chariot racing, and horse racing. Athletes usually competed in the nude, following Greek custom, and winners were awarded

Copyright © Mometrix Media. You have been licensed one copy of this document for personal use only. Any other reproduction or redistribution is strictly prohibited. All rights reserved.
This content is provided for test preparation purposes only and does not imply an endorsement by Mometrix of any particular political, scientific, or religious point of view.

wreaths. Competition became so fierce that city-states treated their winning athletes like heroes, often lavishing rewards upon them.

Public and Private Architecture in Ancient Greece

Greeks believed that public buildings, as they reflected the needs and status of their city-states, were more important than private homes. Most public buildings in the city-states were centered on the acropolis, the hill where the original fort sat. In most city-states, the acropolis came to include the main citadel, the agora (marketplace), various temples honoring gods and goddesses, a gymnasium or stadium, and a theater. A few city-states built palaces for their leaders. In most city-states, however, private homes, even among the wealthy, tended to be very simple, one-story brick buildings with no plumbing systems.

Philip II of Macedon

In the years following the Peloponnesian War and Athens's decline, the northern warrior kingdom of Macedon emerged as a threat to some Greek city-states. During a time of upheaval in Macedon, Thebes tried to take over the kingdom. Young Philip was held hostage in Thebes for three years. During that time he studied Greek culture and military strategies. When Philip became king of Macedon in 359 B.C., he adopted many Greek military strategies and set out to conquer the civilization. First he seized Athenian colonies, and then attacked the mainland. Some Greeks favored Macedonian rule over the prior chaos or a return of Athenian dominance. One by one, the city-states fell to Macedon. At the Battle of Chaeronea, the Macedonians defeated both the Athenians and Thebans, unifying the Greek empire. Philip created the League of Corinth to maintain peace within the empire while he prepared for an invasion of Persia.

Demosthenes in the Age of Philip II

Demosthenes was a skilled Athenian orator who led public opposition to the rise of Philip II of Macedon. While some city-states were surrendering to the Macedonians, Demosthenes encouraged Athenians to hold fast and resist Macedon with all their might. He based his arguments on the need to preserve Athenian democracy. The only way to maintain true freedom for citizens, he argued, was for the city-state to remain independent of outside control. Demosthenes also recommended reforms to make the system even more truly democratic by expanding participation. Over the years he made numerous speeches in defense of the preservation and expansion of democracy. His words are still quoted today. After the assassination of Philip, Demosthenes continued his public assault on Alexander the Great. He faced questionable criminal convictions and exile for his efforts.

Alexander the Great

Alexander became king of the Macedonian empire after his father, Philip II, was assassinated in 336 B.C. Although only 20 years old at the time, Alexander acted as a brilliant general. A great admirer of Greek culture, Alexander set out to unite the entire known world under one Hellenistic empire. He almost succeeded within a very short period of time. By 331 B.C., he controlled Asia Minor, Egypt, Mesopotamia, Persia, Syria, and pressed into India. Alexander the Great's youth, boldness, and brilliance led to his becoming a legend in his own time. His reputation created awe among his contemporaries and only increased after his unexpected death at the age of 33.

Major Events Under the Rule of Alexander the Great

- 336 B.C. — Becomes king of Macedonia
- 335 B.C. — Crushes Theban revolt
- 334 B.C. — Takes control of Persia
- 332 B.C. — Takes control of Gaza
- 331 B.C. — Found city of Alexandria

Copyright © Mometrix Media. You have been licensed one copy of this document for personal use only. Any other reproduction or redistribution is strictly prohibited. All rights reserved.
This content is provided for test preparation purposes only and does not imply an endorsement by Mometrix of any particular political, scientific, or religious point of view.

- 327 B.C. — Marries Persian, Roxanne, to secure cultural ties
- 327 B.C. — Begins invasion of India; series of plots against Alexander begin; he usually responds by murdering conspirators
- 324 B.C. — Troops mutiny at Opis; mutiny reflects loss of support for Alexander, weakened state of troops after years of fighting
- 323 B.C. — After brief illness, Alexander dies mysteriously, leading to speculation that he may have been assassinated

Alexander's Effort to Spread Hellenistic Culture to the Entire World

Alexander the Great spread Hellenistic culture in conquered areas by renaming cities, establishing schools and libraries, and encouraging settlement by Greeks and Persians. Greek became the official language of his empire and its religion became the faith of the empire. The great library at Alexandria served as a repository for Greek literature and spread the influence of Greek thinking as other scholars ventured to study at the library. Most of all, Alexander promoted the notion that Hellenistic culture was the greatest in history. His legendary reputation and efforts helped expand the spread of Hellenistic culture long after his death.

Hellenistic Empire After the Death of Alexander

After Alexander died mysteriously in 323 B.C., several of his generals fought for control of the empire. Another son of Phillip II became king briefly, only to be murdered by the generals. Alexander's only child, a son born after his death, was also crowned, and then executed. In 301 B.C., the generals finally divided the empire into several kingdoms of various sizes. Fighting for dominance continued between these kingdoms for another century. Around 200 B.C., the emerging Romans conquered the kingdom of Macedon and gradually began to take over the entire Hellenistic world.

Golden Age of Hellenistic Culture

"Hellenic" is another word for "Greek." The word "Hellenistic" refers to Greek culture influenced by that of Macedon and Persia. It began to emerge with Philip II of Macedon's conquest of Greece in 338 B.C. and peaked under the reign of Alexander the Great, between 336 B.C. and 323 B.C. Both Philip and Alexander greatly admired Greek culture, adopting many aspects of it and encouraging its spread throughout the world. At no other time in history was Greek culture as influential as during this century. Thanks largely to Alexander's efforts, Hellenistic culture continued to influence other societies long after the fall of the empire.

The Acropolis and It's Reflection of Hellenistic Culture

The Athenian acropolis was built on a walled hillside and still stands today. It represents the finest examples of ancient Greek art, architecture, and culture. It features the Propylaeum, a sacred gateway that opens into the entrance hall. The Acropolis is highlighted by the Parthenon, a temple built to honor the goddess Athena. The white marble Parthenon represents the Greek emphasis on balance, with its perfect proportion of length, width, and height. The structure also utilizes impressive columns typical of many great Hellenistic buildings. It is decorated with numerous sculptures, including a massive rendering of Athena made of ivory and gold. Other important structures in the Acropolis include the Erechtheum, a shrine to gods of agriculture, and the Temple of Athena Nike.

Hellenistic Visual Art

Most Hellenistic art celebrated the human form, reflecting its beauty and seemingly perfect proportions. Artists utilized Greek advances in geometry to improve the symmetry of their representations, reflecting Greek emphasis on balance and moderation. Greeks valued self-

Copyright © Mometrix Media. You have been licensed one copy of this document for personal use only. Any other reproduction or redistribution is strictly prohibited. All rights reserved.
This content is provided for test preparation purposes only and does not imply an endorsement by Mometrix of any particular political, scientific, or religious point of view.

discipline and restraint in their personal conduct. They reflected this in their art by using simple designs and avoiding excess. Figures were often shown in motion, reflecting the Greek emphases on athletic ability and fluidity of motion. Images of both humans and gods were similarly perfect, without flaw, reflecting values the Greeks admired such as strength, intelligence, and grace. Greek art was also intended to reflect pride in the polis. Most art was designed to be placed in public buildings, to be admired by visitors and upheld as a reflection of the city-state. Likewise, much Greek art combined the values and beauty and functionality. Vases, for example, were beautiful, but were also designed to hold water.

Greek Painting

Most original Greek painting that has survived from antiquity can be found on vases. Early Greek artists appear to have been familiar with Egyptian art, imitating many Egyptian styles. Earlier Greek vases focused on images of animals, as Egyptian art did. Over time, more Greek vases showed human forms, reflecting their culture's focus on perfection and beauty of the human body. Other artifacts include funeral steles, carved stones that were made to honor the dead and record significant information about that person's life. They portrayed images of the deceased at work or play. Because many works of art were incorporated into public buildings, artifacts that survive from such buildings reveal Greek art.

Greek Sculptors

- Myron— First major sculptor to combine fluidity of motion with balance of composition; created figures of athletes in action, usually in bronze; major works include the *Discus Thrower*
- Phidias— Oversaw artistic direction of the Parthenon; established popular artistic representations of gods; major works include *Athena* at the Parthenon and *Zeus* at the Temple of Olympia
- Polyclitus — Wrote the *Canon*, a guide to the use of mathematical calculations in sculpting human body; known for bronze sculptures of athletes; major works include the *Spear Bearer* and *Hera,* created in ivory and gold.
- Praxiteles — Focused on sensuality rather than majestic grandeur; experimented with color in sculpture; major works include *Hermes Carrying the Infant Dionysus* and *Aphrodite of Cnidus.*
- Scopas — Expressed emotions in sculptures; major works include *Maenad* and *Pothos;* as architect, oversaw construction of several major temples
- Lysippus — Led art schools at Argos and Sicyon; figures were slender and natural-looking; considered most prolific of Greek artists; most famous works include numerous statues of Alexander the Great

Development of Philosophy

According to tradition, Greeks invented the discipline now known as philosophy. It first arose among a group of thinkers known as the cosmologists, or naturalists, because they were trying to understand how the universe worked. They tried to apply scientific knowledge with creative thinking and logic to explain mysteries unknown to humans. Thales of Miletus was the first philosopher and one of the Seven Wise Men of ancient Greece. He developed the theory that water was the basis of all matter, describing the Earth as a flat disk floating on a cosmic sea. He was followed by Anaximander, who established ideas about the origins of the universe that differed from known mythology. As philosophy spread, thinkers developed rules for logical thinking that guided their work.

Copyright © Mometrix Media. You have been licensed one copy of this document for personal use only. Any other reproduction or redistribution is strictly prohibited. All rights reserved.
This content is provided for test preparation purposes only and does not imply an endorsement by Mometrix of any particular political, scientific, or religious point of view.

MAJOR PHILOSOPHICAL CONTRIBUTIONS

- Socrates — Teacher who emphasized importance of education to personal growth and ethics; invented the Socratic Method, which focused on helping students learn by asking them questions, rather than having them just memorize facts; challenged theories of the Sophists, who controlled Athenian educational system; accusing of corrupting Athenian youth by undermining beliefs about the gods; convicted and executed
- Plato — Student of Socrates who recorded his mentor's teachings; founded the Academy to teach philosophy; expressed ideas in a series of imagined dialogues; ideas included Theory of Forms that emphasized the imperfect nature of the physical world, God as "divine worker," the human soul, reincarnation, and ideal rule by a wise aristocracy.
- Aristotle — Student of Plato who founded school which emphasized diverse study based on logic; believed all forms of government could be equally good, but all could just as easily be tainted by corruption; prolific writer whose ideas became the basis for most of the philosophical thought in western civilization

SCHOOLS OF PHILOSOPHY

These were four main schools of philosophy that emerged during the Hellenistic era.

- Cynicism — taught that people should live simply and naturally without concern for physical pleasure, wealth, or social status; founded by Antisthenes; represented best by Diogenes, who rejected social structures such as the family, willingly lived in poverty, and promoted shameless and outspoken behavior
- Skepticism — taught that all knowledge is uncertain because the universe is in a constant state of flux; promoted constant questioning of scientific, religious, and other beliefs; founded by Pyrrho
- Stoicism — taught that people should not be concerned about their own suffering or that of the world; focus should be on gaining wisdom, which all humans have the ability to obtain through the gift of reason; founded by Zeno
- Epicureanism — taught that people should seek pleasure and avoid pain by limiting their desires; founded by Epicurus

SCIENTIFIC CONTRIBUTIONS

- Democritus — Invented atomic theory which states that all matter is made up of atoms
- Euclid — Developed basic theories of geometry in *Elements*
- Pythagoras — Developed Pythagorean theorem, the basic geometric tool for right triangles
- Archimedes — Calculated value of pi; used mathematics to explain theory of levers; invented compound pulley and Archimedes Screw
- Aristarchus — Determined Earth rotates on axis and that it and other planets orbit the Sun
- Hipparchus — Created calendar based on movement of Sun and Moon; predicted eclipses; established fundamentals of trigonometry
- Eratosthenes — Accurately calculated Earth's circumference

CONTRIBUTIONS TO WESTERN MEDICINE AND BIOLOGY

Hippocrates is considered the father of modern medicine. Prior to his emergence, the treatment of disease was often left to oracles which performed "cures" that left the patient more ill than before. Hippocrates separated medicine from religion, arguing that diseases had natural, not spiritual, causes. He established medicine as a science, conducting studies to develop medical theories. Hippocrates also provided the basis for the Hippocratic Oath which is still used by modern-day doctors. *Aristotle* established the fields of comparative anatomy, taxonomy, and embryology. He

Copyright © Mometrix Media. You have been licensed one copy of this document for personal use only. Any other reproduction or redistribution is strictly prohibited. All rights reserved.
This content is provided for test preparation purposes only and does not imply an endorsement by Mometrix of any particular political, scientific, or religious point of view.

dissected animals to understand more about their structure. He tried to systematically distinguish and categorize different creatures. Aristotle's classification system is still the basis of modern biology. *Herophilus* is considered the father of human anatomy. By dissecting human cadavers, he increased understanding of the structure of the human body. He was the first to realize, for example, that the brain is the center of the nervous system. Herophilus' studies allowed him to improve surgical techniques.

DRAMA

Drama—which in this context means any performed play that involves action and conflict—arose out of the Greek festivals to the gods. As part of the celebrations, poets wrote dramas which were performed for entertainment. The Festival of Dionysia encouraged this art form by incorporating a competition for plays, with the winner being chosen by audience vote. Most city-states incorporated outdoor theaters into their design. The theaters were usually designed for optimal acoustics, with the actors performing in a pitted orchestra area. Every play incorporated a chorus which sung parts of their lines and acted as narrators, commentators, and describers of imagined scenes. Actors used no visual props. Dramas reflected Greek history, culture, and values. Tragedies focused on protagonists who struggled against their fates and usually lost, frequently due to their human failing of hubris. Comedies followed similar plots as tragedies, but contained more humor—often at the expense of famous Greeks— and usually a happy ending

GREEK TRAGEDY

Tragedy:

- Aeschylus. Major works include:
- *Oresteia* trilogy. Includes *Agamemnon, Libation Bearers,* and *Eumenides.* Tells the story of Agamemnon, heroic king in the Trojan War, after he returns from conflict. His domestic woes prove more tragic than the war, scarring future generations.
- *Prometheus Bound.* Includes vivid imagery of stubborn god Prometheus, who is bound in chains to a rock as punishment by Zeus.
- Sophocles. Major works include:
- *Antigone.* Princess faces death in order to retrieve the body of her brother, in defiance of orders by a rigid king.
- *Oedipus the King*. Story of a king who is tricked into marrying his own mother. In shame, he blinds himself to reflect his previous blindness to the truth.
- Euripedes. Major works include:
- *Medea.* Classic commentary on the status of women in Greece. Main character reacts to mistreatment by her husband by killing their children.
- *The Trojan Woman.* Retells story of Trojan War by focusing on its futility rather than glorifying it.

HERODOTUS AND THUCYDIDES

Both writers tried to establish a system for recording historical events, rather than merely trusting oral traditions, myths, and legends. Herodotus is called the Father of History. He wrote a history of the western world based largely on his own travels and studies, as well as a history of the Greco-Persian wars. Herodotus established criteria for accuracy, noting sources from which his information came and distinguishing reported information from his own observations. Thucydides also promoted the need to be accurate and fair in recording history. His *History of the Peloponnesian War* reflected this by trying to present events in an accurate, even tone, rather than glorifying either side. His was also one of the first histories meant to be read and studied rather than spoken orally.

Copyright © Mometrix Media. You have been licensed one copy of this document for personal use only. Any other reproduction or redistribution is strictly prohibited. All rights reserved.
This content is provided for test preparation purposes only and does not imply an endorsement by Mometrix of any particular political, scientific, or religious point of view.

Ancient Near East

Characteristics of Ancient Civilizations

Civilizations are complex societies which contain distinct characteristics beyond those of simple settlements or villages. Most ancient civilizations included the following three characteristics:

- They were able to produce surplus, or extra food, beyond what was needed to maintain their own population growth.
- They included cities or large towns with clearly defined systems of government.
- They had a clear division of labor in which different people carried out specific jobs which benefited the culture as a whole.

In addition to these characteristics, some ancient civilizations also included the following:

- Unique technology or inventions, such as their own calendar for keeping track of seasons and other annual occurrences;
- A system of writing.

Regions Where Civilizations First Emerged

The four regions were:

- the Nile River valley in Egypt
- the Tigris and Euphrates River valley in Mesopotamia
- the Huang and Yangtze River valleys in China
- the Indus River valley in Indian

The four regions all represented large river valleys that provided reliable sources of water for many miles. Each also sustained vast acreage of fertile farming lands which helped societies grow abundant amounts of food. The ability to feed large populations became the basis for all early civilizations. Once the regions developed stable food supplies, towns, governments, and divisions of labor followed. Eventually, all of these groups developed more complex technology, including the use of metals. Most of the civilizations also developed systems of trade with other societies.

Egyptian Civilization

Role of the Nile River in the Ancient Egyptian Civilization

The Nile made the Egyptian civilization possible and served as the center of the civilization. It is the longest river in the world, even though dry desert lands lies not far beyond its banks.. During ancient times, the Nile River provided a natural deterrent to outside invaders. Although it flows south to north, the Nile is also marked by strong north-to-south winds. This made it easy for ancient ships to travel along the river in either direction and eventually helped expand trade along the river and across the Mediterranean Sea. The annual Nile flooding created very fertile soil on the surrounding lands. Although the flooding could be problematic at times, its predictable nature led the Egyptian people to plan their lives around the floods. Eventually, farmers built canals and irrigation systems to expand farmlands for miles beyond the river banks.

Major Egyptian Eras

Upper Egypt contained the southern region headquartered at Thebes, and Lower Egypt contained the northern region headquartered at Memphis. King Menes united the two regions in 3200 B.C.

Copyright © Mometrix Media. You have been licensed one copy of this document for personal use only. Any other reproduction or redistribution is strictly prohibited. All rights reserved.
This content is provided for test preparation purposes only and does not imply an endorsement by Mometrix of any particular political, scientific, or religious point of view.

Afterward, some 30 dynasties, or ruling families, governed Egypt. The periods when Upper and Lower Egypt were united are called kingdoms.

- Old Kingdom—2680 B.C. to 2180 B.C. Social classes developed;
- First Intermediate Period—c. 2180 B.C. to c. 2050 B.C. Marked by civil wars;
- Middle Kingdom— c. 2050 B.C. to 1650 B.C. New pharaohs ushered in stability; Hyksos people arrived with chariots and advanced technology;
- Second Intermediate Period—c. 2180 B.C. to c. 2050 B.C. Hyksos controlled Lower Egypt;
- New Kingdom—c. 1570 B.C. to c. 1080 B.C. Era of strong pharaohs;
- Post imperial era—c. 1080 B.C. to c. 300s B.C. Poor leaders and numerous invasions weakened Egypt until it was no longer under native Egyptian rule.

Government Structure of Ancient Egypt

Pharaohs were the supreme rulers, believed by many to be gods. Ultimately, every person in the kingdom answered to the pharaoh. High priests served as the pharaohs' main advisors. Other central government officials included the vizier (prime minister), chief treasurer, tax collectors, director of public works, and commander of the army. Lands were divided into provinces led by governors. People paid taxes through goods and services. Citizens were sometimes conscripted into government or military service. The Egyptians also used mercenary and slave labor.

Some of the most important New Kingdom pharaohs were:

- Hatshepsut – First female pharaoh; secured borders and expanded trade.
- Thutmose III – Hatshepsut's stepson; brought Egyptian kingdom to height of its power through trade and conquest
- Amenhotep IV – Renamed himself "Akhenaton,"; promoted belief in one god, which led to power struggle with priests
- Ramses II (a.k.a. "Ramses the Great") – Last of strong pharaohs; ordered construction of many great buildings

Accomplishments in the Arts, Science, and Mathematics

The Egyptians developed a system of picture writing called hieroglyphics. They also developed a way to make paper out of the papyrus plant. The Rosetta Stone was discovered around A.D. 1800 and contained passages carved in ancient Greek, hieroglyphics, and other writing systems. Researchers realized that all of the passages said the same thing. Thus, by comparing the hieroglyphic passage to the Greek, researchers could translate what the hieroglyphics meant.

Ancient Egyptians were skilled architects and builders, as evidenced by the pyramids. Ancient Egypt also contained highly skilled sculptors and painters whose works often decorated buildings. The Egyptians developed a lunar calendar, an understanding of astronomy, and a number system based on ten. Largely due to their experiments in mummification, the Egyptians gained an advanced understanding of anatomy and biology.

Religious Beliefs and Customs

Egyptians practiced a system of polytheism that was very fluid across time and place. Although Pharaoh Akhenaton tried to promote the belief in one god, the Sun god Aton, this belief system did not survive beyond Akhenaton's death. Many pharaohs promoted the belief that they themselves were gods, and some villages had their own unique gods. Animals, such as cats, bulls, or scarab

Copyright © Mometrix Media. You have been licensed one copy of this document for personal use only. Any other reproduction or redistribution is strictly prohibited. All rights reserved.
This content is provided for test preparation purposes only and does not imply an endorsement by Mometrix of any particular political, scientific, or religious point of view.

beetles often symbolized gods. In Egyptian mythology, the gods possessed qualities and weaknesses similar to humans. Specific gods included:

- Amon-Re, or Re, the creator or Sun god
- Osiris, judge of the dead and god of the Nile
- Isis, wife of Osiris and goddess of royalty and fertility
- Seth, evil god of the underworld
- Horus, god of the sky
- Thoth, god of the moon

Central to Egyptian religion was a strong belief in an afterlife. This belief influenced the practice of mummification, or preservation of the body; the building of elaborate tombs for royalty and nobility; and the burying of earthly goods within tombs.

SUMER

Ancient Sumer, which developed around 3000 B.C., was divided into independent city-states, each protected by a unique god or goddess. Ur was the primary city-state. Although each city-state usually had a king, the high priests held most of the real power due to the importance of religion to Sumerian life. Nobles made up the third tier of government leadership. Lower priests, merchants, and scholars carried out daily duties for the government. When making important decisions, kings and priests often relied upon divination — the art of telling the future by interpreting signs in sacrificed animal organs, smoke signals, or patterns of oil on water.

EPIC OF GILGAMESH

The *Epic of Gilgamesh* is an ancient Sumerian story that was well-known throughout the Fertile Crescent. Versions have been discovered on tablets written in cuneiform, the ancient wedge form of Sumerian writing. Cuneiform writers used a stylus to draw pictures, representing sounds, into soft clay which later hardened.

The epic relates many aspects of ancient Sumerian life. It tells the story of King Gilgamesh, who built many great ziggurats in his city-state. Ziggurats were stair-stepped temples present in most Sumerian city-states. Gilgamesh was also selfish and greedy, so the gods punished him by killing his best friend and making him go on a long journey in which he had to face his own mortality. Along the way, he met a man who recounted a story of the Great Flood, in which the gods punished sinful humans by flooding the world. One good man was warned and built a boat to survive. The story shares many similarities with the Biblical account of Noah, reflecting widespread awareness of the flood story.

AKKADIAN EMPIRE

The Akkadians were a tribe of Semitic-speaking people who lived in the Mesopotamian city-state of Akkad. Under the leader Sargon, the Akkadians rose up and defeated the Sumerians around 2330 B.C. Sargon relied more on appointees than on the Sumerian priests. He established a complicated bureaucratic structure in which the main goal was to expand economic activity. Sargon also demanded that conquered peoples adopt the Akkadian language, thus expanding its influence. Under Sargon, the Akkadian Empire expanded geographically and became very wealthy. It depended on an expansive road network and introduced a postal system. The leaders who followed Sargon were very weak, fostering infighting and invasion. The Akkadian Empire lasted less than 200 years.

Copyright © Mometrix Media. You have been licensed one copy of this document for personal use only. Any other reproduction or redistribution is strictly prohibited. All rights reserved.
This content is provided for test preparation purposes only and does not imply an endorsement by Mometrix of any particular political, scientific, or religious point of view.

Babylonian Empire

The Babylonians rose to power following the collapse of the Akkadian Empire. Their greatest ruler was Hammurabi, who led from c. 1792 B.C. to 1750 B.C. The code of laws developed under his reign provided a detailed system of justice based on the belief "an eye for an eye," or equal punishment for harm caused during a crime. However, equality of punishment depended upon the social class of the victim and criminal. A wealthy person convicted of harming a poor person could pay a fine in place of receiving physical punishment.

Challenges from Assyrian, Hittite, and Chaldean invaders led the empire to rise and fall several times. Among the later rulers was Nebuchadnezzar II, who ruled from 605 to 562 B.C. He conquered lands and rebuilt the empire to much of its former glory. In 587 B.C., Nebuchadnezzar II destroyed Judah and Jerusalem, ushering in the era of Babylonian Captivity for the Hebrews. The Persians under Cyrus the Great defeated the last Babylonian king in 539 B.C.

Babylonian Culture and Religion

Much of what is known about Babylonian culture comes from the Code of Hammurabi, revealing a highly patriarchal, class-based, society. Parents arranged marriages for children, with fathers having supreme authority. Husbands were allowed to maintain mistresses, but wives were not allowed to commit adultery. Only husbands could petition for divorce. However, women whose husbands had divorced them without just cause could receive financial reimbursement. Women were also allowed to hold a variety of skilled jobs. Most slaves were prisoners of war who worked for the government, farming and building public works. Privately owned slaves usually served as domestic workers. Nobles who owned slaves could claim slaves as their own by cutting off a slave's ear. Enslaved people were allowed to own their own property, run their own businesses, marry free citizens, and purchase their freedom. Many Babylonian religious beliefs were adopted from the Sumerians, including polytheism and the belief in divination.

Hittites

Although their exact origins are unclear, the Hittites were a warrior culture which emerged out of Anatolia around 1750 B.C. Because much of their culture was focused on preparing for warfare, the Hittites were among the earliest cultures to use weapons made from iron, and they developed a smelting process for iron ore. Their legal system only called for the death penalty in rare cases. They also appear to have been fairly tolerant of other religions within their empire. They were among the groups that controlled parts of Babylonia at various times. After looting much of Babylonia's wealth, the Hittites retreated back to the Fertile Crescent. They controlled this region until the invasions of the Sea Peoples around 1200 B.C.

Persians

The Persians were led by a series of kings, such as Medes, Cyrus, Darius, and Xerxes. These kings were all-powerful, but believed in being just and fair, even towards conquered peoples. As their empire expanded, they allowed conquered peoples to retain their own customs, beliefs, and laws. To maintain order across the empire, the rulers appointed regional governors, generals, and tax collectors. A network of secret spies watched over these regional rulers and reported back to the king, allowing for central oversight of the bureaucracy. The Persian government also built an expansive road system to facilitate travel, trade, and communication throughout the empire.

Zoroastrianism

Zoroastrianism was a religious faith that arose under the Persian Empire. Traditional Persian religion was polytheistic, based on worshipping human-like deities who would do specific things for humans. Around 600 B.C., a prophet named Zoroaster arose who focused on the human will to

Copyright © Mometrix Media. You have been licensed one copy of this document for personal use only. Any other reproduction or redistribution is strictly prohibited. All rights reserved.
This content is provided for test preparation purposes only and does not imply an endorsement by Mometrix of any particular political, scientific, or religious point of view.

choose between right and wrong actions. He taught that the universe contained forces for good and for evil that were in constant struggle with one another. Humans could choose to side with good or evil, as evidenced by their actions. Humans who sided with good would be rewarded in the afterlife. Those who chose evil would be punished after death. Zoroaster predicted that eventually the forces of good would win over the forces of evil, at which time the world would end. Many scholars believe that Zoroastrianism influenced Judeo-Christian ethical beliefs.

Israelites

After arriving in the land near Canaan, the Hebrews wandered as a loose confederation of twelve nomadic tribes led by various judges and prophets. The tribes united to fight the Canaanites and Philistines. Around 1020 B.C., they established the Kingdom of Israel, under King Saul. King David followed Saul, defeating many of Israel's enemies and securing control of a new capital city, Jerusalem. Israel reached its height of wealth and power under David's son, King Solomon, who made diplomatic ties and gained lands through marriages to foreign women. Solomon oversaw construction of the First Temple in Jerusalem, and civil war followed Solomon's death. In the 900s B.C., the kingdom split into two — northern Israel, with its capital at Samaria, and southern Judah, with its capital at Jerusalem. The Assyrians defeated Israel in 722 B.C., enslaving the Hebrews. The Chaldeans conquered Judah in 587 B.C., destroying the First Temple. When the Persians took control of these lands, they freed the Hebrews and allowed the building of a Second Temple.

Origins of the Hebrew People Through Moses

According to Biblical tradition, the Hebrews began with a man named Abraham, who lived in the Sumerian city-state of Ur. Abraham rejected polytheism and worshipped one supreme God, who ordered him to lead his household to a new land in Canaan. God promised Abraham that a new nation would rise up from his descendants. Abraham's grandson Jacob, also called "Israel," had twelve sons, from which came the Twelve Tribes of Israel which formed the Hebrew people. Eventually, the Hebrews migrated into Egypt, where they lived peacefully for many years. Between c. 1200 B.C. and c. 800 B.C., the Hebrews suffered harsh enslavement under the Egyptians. The prophet Moses rose up to lead the Exodus, the Hebrew escape from Egyptian slavery. During a period of isolation on Mount Sinai, Moses emerged with the Ten Commandments, fundamental laws to guide the Hebrew people. The Hebrews wandered for many years before returning to the promised land of Canaan, where they eventually founded the Kingdom of Israel.

Beliefs and Customs of Ancient Judaism

Judaism was the religion of the Hebrews and the basis for law and government in Israel and Judah. The foundation of the faith was a belief in one God, referred to as Yahweh or "I am that I am." The Ten Commandments provided the most basic laws of the faith. The Hebrews believed strongly in covenants, or sacred agreements, between themselves and God. They believed they were chosen by God to represent His will on Earth, established through His original covenant with Abraham. Unlike polytheistic gods, Yahweh did not have humanlike weaknesses, but did give humans the free will to choose right or wrong behavior. This belief formed the basis for ethical monotheism, or what became known as Judeo-Christian ethics. Many Biblical stories about the failures of Israel are based on the inability of the Hebrews to maintain their covenant with God. In order to make sure that the Hebrews remembered their covenant, Judaism developed many customs and rituals designed to control people's behaviors and set them apart from other cultures.

Assyrians

The Assyrians were a Semitic-speaking people from what is now Turkey. They ruled various parts of Mesopotamia at different times. The height of their power came between c. 900 B.C. and c. 650 B.C., when the Assyrian Empire included all of Mesopotamia, Syria, Palestine, and the Nile River

Copyright © Mometrix Media. You have been licensed one copy of this document for personal use only. Any other reproduction or redistribution is strictly prohibited. All rights reserved.
This content is provided for test preparation purposes only and does not imply an endorsement by Mometrix of any particular political, scientific, or religious point of view.

valley. The Assyrians were a warrior society, thus many of their technological achievements aided them in battle. They used horses and chariots in combat, and originated the use of cavalry in warfare. The discovery of the Nimrud Lens in 1850 suggests the possibility that the Assyrians built telescopes or at least magnifying glasses.

Fertile Crescent

Mesopotamia was the region between the Tigris and Euphrates rivers. The rivers flooded often, making the surrounding soil very fertile for farming. Bordered by the Taurus Mountains to the northwest, the Mediterranean Sea to the southwest, the Syrian Desert to the south, the Zagros Mountains to the northeast, and the Persian Gulf to the southeast, the strip of the most fertile land formed the shape of a sideways crescent, with the tips facing southward. Due to the fertile lands, humans began to develop agriculture in this area by at least 8000 B.C.

Phoenicians

The Phoenicians did not establish a large land empire, yet they became the greatest seafaring traders of the ancient world. They created advances in sailing technology which enabled them to reach distant shores, possibly as far as Britain and the west coast of Africa. The Phoenicians established a network of trade colonies which soon grew into major cities and countries, including the colonies of Carthage, Sicily, Sardinia, Malta, and even Cadiz, in what is now Spain. Beginning with items they acquired through trade, the Phoenicians made great advances in metalworking and glass-blowing. Using the shellfish murex, they invented the much-prized purple dye that lent color to royal clothing. Their longest-lasting contribution was the invention of the Phoenician alphabet. This character writing system formed the basis for most alphabets that would later be used in the western world.

Lydians

The Lydians of Asia Minor were traders who made contact with many different peoples. Beginning around 600 B.C., they were also one of the earliest civilizations to coin their own money. Their first coins were small crescent-shaped pieces made out of gold and silver. Soon the Lydians were running the first true money economy, in which the coins represented the value of certain goods. The first retail stores may also have originated in Lydia. The Lydian society did not last long, but through their trade ties and conquests by others, the Lydians passed along the concept of using coins to the Greeks and Persians, who then carried them to other peoples.

Copyright © Mometrix Media. You have been licensed one copy of this document for personal use only. Any other reproduction or redistribution is strictly prohibited. All rights reserved.
This content is provided for test preparation purposes only and does not imply an endorsement by Mometrix of any particular political, scientific, or religious point of view.

Ancient Rome

Facts of the Latins

- Peoples who moved into the west-central Italian area called Latium, before 700s B.C.
- Probably descended from Indo-Europeans
- Culturally influenced by southern Italian tribes and Villanovans of Etruria
- Established villages along the Tiber River
- United to create city of Rome, c. 753 B.C.
- Language provided basis for that of the Roman Empire
- Continued to be influential in outer Latium region after losing Rome to Etruscans
- Formed alliance called the Latin League to influence policies in Rome
- Divisions grew as Rome established a culture distinct from Latin League members
- 300s B.C. Rome defeated Latins, took control of Latium, and dissolved Latin League

Rome

Geographic Location

Rome sits in the middle of the Italian Peninsula, a boot-shaped piece of land surrounded by the Adriatic, Ionian, Tyrrhenian, and Mediterranean seas. This was an ideal location for seafaring trade and, eventually, for controlling a vast empire that stretched from the Caspian Sea in the east to Spain in the west. The Apennine Mountains along the eastern side of the peninsula were easy to traverse. However, the northern Alps were difficult to cross, helping protect Rome from northern enemies, yet making it more difficult for Romans to travel north. Surrounded almost entirely by seas, the peninsula was vulnerable to attack by strong navies.

The city itself was built on Palatine Hill, one of seven close-fitting hills along the narrowest point of the Tiber River, going inland from the west coast. This location helped protect Rome from sea-based invasions. The Tiber provided a constant supply of water, but was easy to traverse for travel and trade.

Etruscans

The Etruscans represented a kingdom from northern Italy who began seizing control of Italian lands to limit Greek expansion. They took over Rome from the Latins in the mid-600s BC. At that time, Rome was more of a community of villages than an organized city. The Etruscans, who were skilled artisans and engineers, organized the city into a unified urban area by improving roads and drainage systems, fortifying walls, and building sewer systems. As the Etruscans continued to challenge Greek dominance in the Mediterranean, the population and trade ties of Rome grew. An uprising among the Romans drove the Etruscans from the city in 509 B.C., and in 475 B.C., a combined force of Latins and Greeks drove them completely from Latium. The Etruscans never regained their political power, but their restructuring of Rome made it the major city it would continue to be for centuries.

Republican Form of Government

For many years after its founding, Rome was ruled by kings advised by a noble senate. According to legend, most of the kings ruled wisely and justly. In 534 B.C., Lucius Tarquinius (a.k.a. Tarquin) became the seventh king of Rome. Tarquin was an arrogant despot who added the title Superbus (meaning "the proud") to his name. He established a reign of terror, openly executing his political enemies, including members of the Senate. After Tarquin ordered his son to rape Lucretia, the wife of a senator (an event that led to her suicide), other senators organized a popular uprising that

Copyright © Mometrix Media. You have been licensed one copy of this document for personal use only. Any other reproduction or redistribution is strictly prohibited. All rights reserved.
This content is provided for test preparation purposes only and does not imply an endorsement by Mometrix of any particular political, scientific, or religious point of view.

exiled Tarquin. The Etruscan leader Porsenna, who had helped defeat Tarquin, expected to be crowned the new king, but the Romans soon drove all the Etruscans out of the city. The senators who had led the uprising rejected monarchy altogether and created a republic in which they would have the majority of power.

Organizational Structure of the Roman Republic

The republic included three basic levels:

- Senate — the most powerful level; controlled public treasury and foreign policy; sometimes served as judiciary; in times of emergency could approve appointment of dictator for a six month period; members appointed by consuls, but served for life
- Magistrates — included the following:
- Consuls — two chief executives; served one-year terms; led government and army with advice from Senate; could appoint dictators; one consul could veto the other, establishing principle of checks and balances; nominated by Senate, approved by Centuriate
- Praetors — oversaw legal system in times of peace; managed army in times of war; established precedents for civil law; numbers varied over time
- Censors — appointed candidates to Senate; enforced Roman moral code; registered citizens by wealth
- Assemblies — Two major ones, both made up of citizens (adult men):
- Centuriate assembly — Voted on issues involving war or peace treaties; elected magistrates involved with military issues
- Tribal assembly — Elected officials overseeing nonmilitary affairs; handled some legislative decisions; served as criminal court

Conflict of the Orders

Causes — Initially in the republic, power was vested only in the wealthy landowning class called patricians. The majority plebeians, landless farmers and workers, could vote, but not hold public office. In time, they came to resent this unequal system. In 494 B.C., the plebeians launched the first of several protests to emphasize their importance. When the city was under threat from neighboring forces, the plebeians launched a strike and left the city rather than protect it. The plebeians returned after republican leaders agreed to establish a plebeian tribune.

Effects — Through further protests, the plebeians secured more political rights. Around 450 B.C., they forced the patricians to write down the Roman legal code on the Twelve Tablets and place them on public display. After 342 B.C., one of the consuls always had to be a plebeian. The Conflict of the Orders resulted in a more democratic government, with more power for the plebeians. In time, it weakened the social division between landowners and non-landowners, establishing a new level of nobility.

Punic Wars

Causes — The Punic Wars were three conflicts fought between the Romans and Carthaginians (once part of the Phoenician, or Punic, empire) over control of trade in the Mediterranean. By the mid-200s B.C., the Romans controlled all of southern Italy, threatening Carthage's trade colony on Sicily. Rome desired to expand its trade network across the seas, but feared resistance from powerful Carthage. The First Punic War was sparked in 264 B.C. when Carthage intervened in a dispute between the Sicilian cities of Messina and Syracuse and established a base on the island. Roman troops forced Carthage to withdraw, and then continued to attack other Carthaginian colonies.

Copyright © Mometrix Media. You have been licensed one copy of this document for personal use only. Any other reproduction or redistribution is strictly prohibited. All rights reserved.
This content is provided for test preparation purposes only and does not imply an endorsement by Mometrix of any particular political, scientific, or religious point of view.

Effects — During the wars Rome, which previously had no navy, developed a powerful all-sea fighting force. Carthage lost all three costly wars, and thus its dominance, as did its ally Macedonia. By the end of the wars, Carthage was completely destroyed, and Rome was unquestionably the most powerful empire in the Mediterranean region.

Major Events

- 264 B.C. First Punic War began when Carthage intervened in Sicilian dispute.
- 241 B.C. First Punic War ended with Carthage requesting a peace treaty; Carthage gave up Sicily and paid substantial reparations.
- 218 B.C. Second Punic War began when Hannibal's army crossed the Alps and attacked Rome from the north.
- 204 B.C. Roman forces attacked northern Africa, directly threatening Carthage and forcing Hannibal home to defend the city-state.
- 202 B.C. Scipio led a Roman victory over Hannibal's troops at the Battle of Zama, ending the Second Punic War; Carthage gave up its navy, Spanish colonies, and more money in reparations, but remained independent.
- 197 B.C. Rome defeated Carthage's ally, Macedon.
- 149 B.C. Third Punic War began when Rome invaded Carthage with the intention to destroy it.
- 146 B.C. The Romans razed Carthage, sold its citizens into slavery, and forbid any new settlement on the site.

Inadequacy of the Roman Republic

For efficiency during the wars, more power had been vested in the patrician-dominated Senate. As Roman landholdings expanded, the Republic relied upon a loosely organized provincial system which fostered corruption. The residents of the provinces had no political rights. With little oversight from Republican leaders, provincial governors and tax collectors abused the provincial residents, fostering widespread resentment. Destruction of farmland caused by the wars (especially the Second Punic Wars) led to widespread food shortages and increased poverty among families of returning soldiers, many of whom filled the streets of Rome. Business leaders and landowners called equites took advantage of the crisis to gain more power and wealth for themselves. As class conflict increased, the Republican leadership seemed incapable of responding to the impending crisis. Instead, they tried to distract the masses with food handouts and free public entertainment.

Social War

Causes — During the Punic Wars many cities in the Italian Peninsula had allied themselves with Rome and provided troops, money, and supplies. After the victory, they wanted to share in the rewards. They also wanted to expand their role in the Roman Empire by having full rights of citizenship and roles in the Roman government. In 91 B.C., Marcus Livius Drusus proposed offering citizenship to all residents of the Italian Peninsula. Not only did the Senate reject this proposal, but Drusus was assassinated soon afterward. In response, the noncitizen cities joined forces to attack Rome, an effort that became known as the Social War.

Effects — What was effectively a civil war resulted in widespread destruction and loss of life. Rome suppressed the rebellion, but the Senate recognized it would have to make concessions to ensure permanent peace. The Senate expanded citizenship rights and government jobs to residents of other cities, broadening the concept of Roman national identity to all natives of the Italian Peninsula.

Copyright © Mometrix Media. You have been licensed one copy of this document for personal use only. Any other reproduction or redistribution is strictly prohibited. All rights reserved.
This content is provided for test preparation purposes only and does not imply an endorsement by Mometrix of any particular political, scientific, or religious point of view.

Significant People

- Tiberius Gracchus — one of two brothers known as the Gracchi; elected tribune in 133 B.C.; sympathetic to economic plight of farmer-soldiers; proposed land reforms; popular with common people, but seen as a threat to Senate; murdered by political opponents
- Gaius Gracchus — one of two brothers known as the Gracchi; elected tribune in 123 and 122 B.C.; attempted reforms including government sale of low-cost food to the poor; reforms angered Senate; killed in protest riots
- Gaius Marius — consul elected in 107 B.C.; popular leader; replaced drafted army with paid volunteer troops
- Lucius Cornelius Sulla — consul elected in 88 B.C.; after clashing with political enemies (including Gaius Marius), led army to attack Rome; ruled as dictator from 82 B.C. to 79 B.C.; expanded Senate to 300 members; established precedent of using military force to control Senate

Julius Caesar

Julius Caesar, nephew of Gaius Marius, was a popular general and public speaker. In 60 B.C., he formed the First Triumvirate, a political alliance with Gaius Pompey and Licinius Crassus. With their support, Caesar increased his military power by taking control of the Roman army in Gaul. Under his command, the Romans secured Gaul, and Caesar insured the loyalty of his troops. After Crassus died in 53 B.C., Pompey attempted to recall Caesar to Rome without his army. Instead, Caesar defiantly led his troops across the Rubicon, sending Pompey into Greece. Caesar followed, defeated Pompey, then invaded Egypt and secured an alliance with Cleopatra. He returned to Rome in 46 B.C. as a conquering hero. Caesar increased his public popularity through reforms such as expanding the size of the Senate, while actually diluting its power. After the Senate declared him dictator for life, opponents and some former allies came to believe the all-powerful leader had to be stooped. Caesar's opponents organized his assassination on the Ides of March, 44 B.C.

Augustus Caesar

In his will, Julius Caesar named his nephew Octavian as his successor. Many of the conspirators who killed Caesar opposed the ascension of this teenager and used their own armies to seize control of outer provinces. Octavian allied himself with Marcus Lepidus and Marc Antony to defeat the conspirators and secure the empire. Together they formed the Second Triumvirate. After Lepidus retired, Octavian and Marc Antony, now allied with Cleopatra, divided control of the empire. Octavian led the west, Antony the east. Wise Octavian soon won the trust of the people and of the Senate, which authorized him to seize control of the eastern empire. After Octavian's fleet defeated Antony's at the Battle of Actium, both Antony and Cleopatra committed suicide. Octavian launched a series of military expeditions to expand the borders of the Roman Empire, thus ensuring protection for the Italian Peninsula. In 27 B.C., the Senate awarded Octavian the title of Augustus, meaning "revered one." Afterward, Rome was be ruled by emperors.

Pax Romana

The term means "Roman Peace." It describes the 200-year period between the reigns of Augustus and Marcus Aurelius, when the empire experienced relative peace (from major foreign invasions and civil wars) and prosperity. It is considered the "golden age" of the Roman Empire. During this time, the expansion of Roman laws and presence of the army brought stability to the provinces. Rome built an extensive network of strong roads and bridges to improve communication, trade, and troop movements. Roman arts and sciences also flourished during this period. The Pax Romana allowed for the expansion of Roman culture and the Romanization of western civilization.

Copyright © Mometrix Media. You have been licensed one copy of this document for personal use only. Any other reproduction or redistribution is strictly prohibited. All rights reserved.
This content is provided for test preparation purposes only and does not imply an endorsement by Mometrix of any particular political, scientific, or religious point of view.

Julio-Claudian Emperors

- Tiberius (A.D. 14–37): Initially wise, but became cruel and mentally unstable; used Praetorian Guard to intimidate Senate; spent last years living on Capri, allegedly engaging in debauchery and violence, while leaders of Guard led Rome; murdered by Caligula's supporters
- Caligula (A.D. 37–41): United all armies under his power; murdered indiscriminately; promoted own divinity; aspired to marry his sister; widely believed insane before he was murdered by Praetorian Guard
- Claudius (A.D. 41–54): Tough, but generally wise ruler; oversaw conquest of Britain and North Africa; improved provincial justice and administration; expanded Roman religion and public works; poisoned by wife to allow ascension of Nero
- Nero (A.D. 54–68): First five years marked by reforms to expand justice and end corruption; decline perhaps due to mental illness; ordered deaths of mother and wife; engaged in debauchery; infamous for allegedly "fiddling while Rome burned" in A.D. 64; reputed to have persecuted Christians; committed suicide amid revolt and potential assassination

Flavian Emperors

Following Nero's death, the empire experienced a struggle for power, mainly among its military leaders. In one year, five different people served as emperor, each dying violently. The three emperors of the non-noble Flavian family restored order and a line of succession.

- Vespasian (A.D. 69–79) Carefully built foreign and military alliances through the string of emperors; used military to defeat other claimants to throne; stabilized empire; suppressed Jewish rebellion; rebuilt Rome to greater than pre-fire glory; massive works included Forum and Colosseum; one of few emperors considered to have improved his performance during his reign
- Titus (A.D. 79–81) Handsome, popular leader; rewarded supporters with monetary gifts; completed building of Colosseum; sudden death stunned empire; possibly murdered by Domitian
- Domitian (A.D. 81–96) Unpopular with public and most members of government, but secured support of military with salary increases; clashed with Senate; imposed tyrannical rule over public officials; late in reign reputed to have stolen widely from the public; murdered by palace insiders

Good Emperors

Wise leaders who avoided crises and violence by adopting and naming the person whom they wanted to succeed them as emperor.

- Nerva (A.D. 96–98) Restored rule by Julio-Claudian family; rejected tyranny of Domitian; restored positions of wise elder statesmen; instituted agrarian and charitable reforms
- Trajan (A.D. 98–117) Of Spanish birth, first non-Italian-born emperor; expanded reforms to help the poor; ended corruption and misuse of military force; expanded public works within Rome and throughout the empire
- Hadrian (A.D. 117–138) Strong general; admired by army; personally visited much of the empire; ordered new public improvements, including Hadrian's Wall in Britain, as needed to protect the empire's population from invaders
- Antoninus Pius (A.D.138–161) Long-lived, but relatively quiet reign; suppressed some revolts in provinces; built the Antonine Wall to further protect Britain

Copyright © Mometrix Media. You have been licensed one copy of this document for personal use only. Any other reproduction or redistribution is strictly prohibited. All rights reserved.
This content is provided for test preparation purposes only and does not imply an endorsement by Mometrix of any particular political, scientific, or religious point of view.

- Marcus Aurelius (A.D. 161–180) Intellectual ruler; follower of Stoicism; believer in rule of law; co-ruled with Lucius Verus for eight years; experienced beginning of tribal invasions; tried unsuccessfully to expand empire's borders

Legend of Romulus and Remus

According to legend, two brothers, Numitor and Amulius, descendents of the Trojans, struggled for power over an Italian tribe. Amulius overthrew his brother and forced Numitor's daughter Rhea to become a Vestal Virgin, hopefully ensuring she would never produce a royal heir. The god Mars then impregnated Rhea, who gave birth to twins Romulus and Remus. The gods protected the twins when Amulius ordered them drowned. A she-wolf suckled them until the boys were adopted by a kind herdsman. The twins grew up to overthrow Amulius and restore Numitor, but struggled themselves over which would inherit the throne. Romulus won the fight by killing his brother and founding Rome.

The legend reflects a strong link between Greek and Roman cultures, establishing the Romans as descendents of the Greeks and Rome as a favored city among the gods. The story mimics many elements of Greek mythology. Images of the she-wolf suckling Romulus and Remus became very common throughout Roman art.

Influence of Greek Culture on the Romans

Because of their close proximity (including colonies on the southern Italian Peninsula) and the spread of Greek culture throughout the Mediterranean region (especially during the reign of Alexander the Great), the Romans adopted many aspects of Greek culture. The Roman religion mirrored that of the Greeks, simply Latinizing many names for the gods, such as Greek Zeus/Roman Jupiter. The Romans also adapted many Greek myths to their own culture. Roman statesmen admired ancient Athenian leaders and tried to emulate them. They also admired Greek literature, art, and architecture. The Roman educational system included a foundation in classical Greek writings. Most Roman intellectuals knew Greek as well as they knew Latin. Roman artists and architects began their works with the models of ancient Greece. Culturally, there was little in Rome that was not in some way descended from Hellenistic culture.

Roman Military

The army provided Rome's true strength. Training was brutal, and discipline was very strict. During the early era of the republic, all male landowners were required to serve in the army upon reaching adulthood. Later, noncitizen units, auxilia, were organized. During the Punic Wars, Rome added a navy. Troops were divided as such:

- legion — made up of 6,000 soldiers (legionnaires), divided into:
- cohorts — 10 groups of 600 soldiers, divided into:
- centuria — 6 groups of 100 soldiers, each led by a centurion

After Gaius Marius introduced the volunteer army, the political role of the military increased and soldiers' motives changed. During the Imperial Era, generals began to rely more on professional soldiers and mercenaries, who fought for wealth rather than to protect their own homes. As such, legions often became corrupt pawns in battles for political power more than protectors of the people and nation.

Treatment of Conquered Peoples

To maintain order, the Romans allowed some cultural independence to conquered peoples. However, all people living under Roman rule were expected to be loyal to Rome. At first, no one

Copyright © Mometrix Media. You have been licensed one copy of this document for personal use only. Any other reproduction or redistribution is strictly prohibited. All rights reserved.
This content is provided for test preparation purposes only and does not imply an endorsement by Mometrix of any particular political, scientific, or religious point of view.

other than those born in Rome could become citizens. Later, citizenship was extended to residents of the Italian Peninsula, and partial citizenship was granted to those in nearby lands. Partial citizens had some rights, but could not vote. Residents of frontier lands were considered noncitizens. They had no political rights as Romans, but were expected to follow Roman laws, pay taxes, and provide land and supplies for the public good. The tax system for the provinces was different than for the city of Rome, placing a heavier burden on many noncitizens.

Structures of the City of Rome

Rome was a well-planned city which was expanded by many emperors to reflect the strength and power of the empire. As in ancient Greece, the most effort was spent on lavish public buildings, with exteriors more elaborate than interiors. Designs included the use of arches, columns, and concrete. Major structures included:

- The Forum — Central area around which other major structures were built; modeled after Athenian Acropolis; site of most public business during the republic
- Circus Maximus — first and largest hippodrome for public entertainment; U-shaped
- Pantheon — Huge domed temple; unique for its elaborate interior design
- Colosseum — Freestanding amphitheater; infamous as site of blood sports and public executions
- Flavian Palace — Lavish structure used more for government ceremonies than as an imperial home
- House of Vestal Virgins — Home of revered high priestesses who maintained Temple of Vesta
- Aqueducts — Massive waterworks system; finest example of Roman engineering
- Baths — Numerous elaborate sites for public bathing; became popular gathering sites for meetings and entertainment

Slavery in the Roman Empire

As the empire expanded, so too did its reliance upon slavery. Initially, most slaves were captives of war. Over time, they played an increasingly important role in the Roman economy, doing most of the agricultural work and manual labor, such as construction of public buildings. Many slaves also performed skilled services, domestic work, and even ran markets. Later, some slaves served as soldiers in the Roman army. Their role in the economy freed other laborers for military service needed to expand and protect the empire's borders. Officials and war heroes were often awarded with personal slaves, making ownership a sign of status. Treatment of slaves varied, but was often humiliating and brutal. The slave revolt led by Spartacus in 73-71 B.C. reflected their disgruntlement. Although successfully suppressed, the rebellion fueled distrust between slaves and freedmen. Some scholars have argued that dependence upon slave labor weakened the Roman Empire by preventing the formation of a free working class or middle class and furthering corruption and debauchery among the wealthy.

Roman Family Life

The family was considered the center of Roman culture, reflected in the veneration of lares, or household deities. The father was head of the household, taking part in public works and making most major decisions. Females managed the household. Women were not citizens, but did have some rights, including the right to own property. Both boys and girls were educated, with wealthier families sending their children to group schools. Only teenage boys attended secondary schools. Girls usually married around age 14 to an older man selected by their fathers.

Copyright © Mometrix Media. You have been licensed one copy of this document for personal use only. Any other reproduction or redistribution is strictly prohibited. All rights reserved.
This content is provided for test preparation purposes only and does not imply an endorsement by Mometrix of any particular political, scientific, or religious point of view.

The Romans placed great importance on Vesta, the goddess of hearth and family. As such, one rare opportunity for women was the priestess order of the six Vestal Virgins. Girls between the ages of six and ten were carefully selected for the order, in which they served for 30 years. Although allowed to marry when their terms ended, few did. The Vestal Virgins obtained positions of status and independence allowed for few Roman women.

Entertainment in the Roman Empire

The Romans became famous (then infamous) for their adulation of amusement and entertainment. Initially, in venues like the Circus Maximus, Romans enjoyed many of the same types of distractions, which special emphasis on sports, theater, and religious festivals, as the Greeks. In time, however, entertainment for its own sake became more common. The wealthy and poor alike enjoyed performances such as plays and circuses, competitions such as chariot races, and blood combat, such as deadly gladiator battles. Even public executions were considered entertainment. Critics complained that such amusements ("bread and circuses") kept the public distracted from real problems facing the empire. Some also felt the entertainment led to corruption, such as the gluttonous banquets and debased orgies in which the wealthy indulged. To many historians, the expansion of entertainment marked a decline in morality and discipline within the Roman Empire, contributing to its decline.

Roman Contributors to Literature

Literature:

- Ennius, poet and dramatist; considered founder of Roman literature; wrote epic poem *Annales* about Roman history
- Livy, historian; known for great storytelling style
- Virgil, poet; wrote epic the *Aeneid,* story of Rome's legendary founding and mission to civilize the world
- Horace, lyric poet; wrote numerous odes and epistles, often satirical in nature
- Ovid, poet; wrote *Metamorphosis,* massive retelling of numerous ancient myths and legends in poetic form
- Tacitus, historian; wrote *Histories* and *Annals,* covering era from A.D. 14 to 96; criticized growing class divisions and extreme lifestyles of the rich
- Plutarch, wrote *Parallel Lives,* collection of Greek and Roman biographies

Romans and Jews

Most Jews became part of the empire when the Romans took control of Judaea in A.D. 6. In order to maintain the support of Jewish leaders, the Romans allowed Jews to freely practice their religion. Some Jewish factions opposed Roman rule, believing that God meant for only Jews to control Jerusalem. The Zealots advocated revolt against the Romans and the establishment of a Jewish state. Some Jews came to believe that a prophesied Messiah would deliver them from Roman rule. Between A.D. 66 and 70, Jews staged a massive revolt against the Romans, which resulted in the sacking of Jerusalem and destruction of the Second Temple. In A.D. 135, the Romans put down a final Jewish revolt and banished the Jews from Jerusalem. Exiled from the city, they established Jewish settlements in the surrounding areas.

Life and Message of Jesus

Based on Biblical and other accounts, Jesus was an Israelite born around 6 B.C. who grew up in the town of Nazareth. Around A.D. 27, he began to travel around the Judean countryside, performing miracles and teaching to the people. Jesus extended the tenets of the Old Testament, arguing that the faith had become so legalistic and ritualistic that Jewish leaders had lost sight of its main

Copyright © Mometrix Media. You have been licensed one copy of this document for personal use only. Any other reproduction or redistribution is strictly prohibited. All rights reserved.
This content is provided for test preparation purposes only and does not imply an endorsement by Mometrix of any particular political, scientific, or religious point of view.

message. He emphasized the fundamental belief in one God and duty to love other people. His message emphasized forgiveness and inclusion for all people, even non-Jews. As such, he often consorted with people rejected by others in the Jewish community, including corrupt tax collectors and Roman soldiers. Most importantly, Jesus emphasized his own divinity and the necessity of believing in him to attain eternal life. After three years of teaching, Jesus was arrested; tried before Pontius Pilate, the Roman governor of Judaea; and crucified. His followers believe he rose from the dead three days after his death.

Spread of Christianity after the Death of Jesus

After Jesus's death, his closest followers travelled throughout the countryside spreading his message. The proponents initially viewed the faith as a movement within Judaism, and thus focused their message on Jews. Soon, however, they began to spread their message to Gentiles. Although the Apostle Peter is considered the first leader of the Christian church, Paul was the follower most responsible for spreading the faith. Paul was originally a Jewish leader named Saul who persecuted Jews. After a religious experience on the road to Damascus, he converted and changed his name to Paul. Afterward, he traveled extensively, founding and advising churches throughout Palestine, Greece and Macedonia. The movement spread quickly throughout much of the Roman Empire.

Influence of Constantine and Theodosius

When Christianity first began, Roman authorities ignored the movement, considering it a harmless sect of Judaism. As it gained converts, some Roman officials began to view the movement as a threat to the political authority of the empire. As a result, they persecuted and sometimes executed Christians, which only made martyrs out of the dead. During the violence and chaos that followed the era of the Five Good Emperors, many people converted to Christianity as a means of comfort and hope. As the faith grew in popularity, it became more difficult for the empire to suppress it. Emperor Constantine formally accepted Christianity in A.D. 312, and promoted its spread throughout the empire as a stabilizing force. Constantine himself was baptized before his death in 337. In 391, Emperor Theodosius, fighting supporters of paganism, made Christianity the official religion of the empire

Council of Nicaea

In the fourth century A.D., Arius, a Christian preacher in Libya, argued that Jesus was an eminently high and powerful creature, but not divine like the Father. To the church fathers, this was heresy, and to refute this statement, the First Council of Nicaea was held in 325. A new statement of faith was adopted for the church, and over many decades, was revised to counter additional heresies. The eventual wording, besides restating certain aspects of the Apostles' Creed, emphasized that Jesus was of the same substance or essence as the Father, being begotten but not created. A major controversy of the council was whether to use the term for "same substance" (*homoousios*) or "similar substance" (*homoiousios*), where the terms differed only by one letter, specifically one iota; to preserve the unity of Christ and the Father, the term for "same substance" was used in the creed. This Nicene Creed remains an official statement of faith for Western and Eastern Christians.

Romans and Goths

The Goths consisted of two Eastern European groups, the Ostrogoths and Visigoths, who began to move into Roman territory after being pushed out of their own lands by the Huns. The Romans accepted the Goths, but mistreated them, leading to widespread starvation among the tribe. In A.D. 378, the Goths launched a revolt, easily defeating the Roman forces at Adrianople and killing the eastern emperor Valens. It was a rare defeat that marked the weakening of the once-mighty Roman army. Roman officials allowed the Goths to establish their own autonomous communities in

Copyright © Mometrix Media. You have been licensed one copy of this document for personal use only. Any other reproduction or redistribution is strictly prohibited. All rights reserved.
This content is provided for test preparation purposes only and does not imply an endorsement by Mometrix of any particular political, scientific, or religious point of view.

exchange for the Goths serving in the Roman army. Further mistreatment resulted in new revolts and the sacking of Rome in A.D. 410.

Vandals

While the Romans were busy defending their capital from the Goths, the Vandals took advantage of the situation and invaded Gaul. The Vandals were a warrior tribe noted for massive looting and destruction of property wherever they raided, spawning the terms *vandal* and *vandalism.* They pushed through Spain, then North Africa. Sensing Roman weakness, they began attacking and taking control of Roman territories. The Vandals engaged a pirate fleet to plunder Roman merchant ships. They finally invaded and attacked Rome in A.D. 455. Though the Vandals only held Rome for a few weeks before fleeing, they escaped with a great deal of wealth and valuable artwork.

Huns

The Huns were a band of fierce warriors from east of the Volga River who began to move westward in the A.D. 300s. As they began taking control of Eastern Europe, the Huns drove groups, such as the Goths into the Roman Empire, escalating conflicts which weakened the empire. By the mid-400s, under the leadership of Attila, the Huns set out to conquer the Roman Empire by attacking Gaul. The Romans allied themselves with their former enemy, the Visigoths, against the Huns, stopping Attila's army at the Battle of the Catalaunian Plains. The Huns continued to attack Roman cities and villages, but their threat weakened after the death of Attila in 453.

Political State After the Five Good Emperors

Following the death of Marcus Aurelius in A.D. 180, leadership passed to his teenage son, Commodus. The youthful leader emulated the poor leadership and debauched behavior of Julio-Claudian emperors, seeming to care more about his personal pleasures than the good of the nation. After Commodus's murder in A.D. 192, violence once again became the normative method of imperial selection. The empire suffered from a series of poor rulers distracted by infighting. As political insecurity reigned in Rome, the empire became vulnerable to attacks from outside forces. Economic troubles led to inflation, a decline of wealth for the public treasury, and social instability that threatened the future of imperial rule.

Diocletian and Constantine

Diocletian and Constantine brought order back to Rome, stabilizing the empire and probably delaying its final collapse. Diocletian rose to prominence as a general and was named emperor in A.D. 284. Arguing that the empire was too large for one leader to manage, he named Maximian as co-emperor and appointed Galerius and Constantius as caesars, or assistants. Diocletian tried to stabilize the economy by instituting wage and price controls. He also used the force of his army to restore order to the frontiers and drive out the invading forces.

When Diocletian and Maximian retired in A.D. 305, their consuls were promoted to co-emperors. When Constantius died the following year, his son, Constantine, was named as his replacement. Galerius refused to recognize Constantine, leading to another battle for power, which Constantine won. Upon becoming sole emperor in A.D. 324, Constantine tried to restore order by naming Christianity as the faith of the empire and moving the capital to Constantinople.

Copyright © Mometrix Media. You have been licensed one copy of this document for personal use only. Any other reproduction or redistribution is strictly prohibited. All rights reserved.
This content is provided for test preparation purposes only and does not imply an endorsement by Mometrix of any particular political, scientific, or religious point of view.

Organizational Structure of the Provinces

During the last two centuries of the empire, Romans maintained control over the provinces through several layers of bureaucracy, overseen by officials in the two administrative centers at Rome and Constantinople. The levels included:

- Civil Authority
- Four Prefectures
- Gauls (overseen by Rome)
- Italy (overseen by Rome)
- Illyricum (overseen by Constantinople)
- Orient (overseen by Constantinople)
- Diocese — formed prefectures ruled by vicars
- Provinces — formed diocese; ruled by governors
- Military Authority
- Mobile Army and Frontier Guards
- Masters of Soldiers — reported to emperor
- Masters of Infantry — reported to emperor
- Masters of Cavalry — reported to emperor

Split of Eastern and Western Roman Empire

Diocletian set the precedent for splitting the empire when he established two centers for civil authority and split rule of the empire between himself and a co-emperor. Constantine reunited imperial rule, through in practice the administrative divisions remained. In the years immediately following Constantine's death in A.D. 337, the Roman Empire remained stable, though corrupt. Over the years instability and poor leadership began to overtake the empire. Gradually, the civil authority headquartered in Constantinople proved more adept than the leaders centered in Rome. The two realms evolved into a de facto split empire, sometimes with different emperors. The western empire continued to decline in power, wealth, and stability. Increasingly, the two realms also became more divided culturally. After the death of Emperor Theodosius, the division between the two empires remained permanent.

Decline of the Roman Empire

Contribution of Economic Crises

The costs of running the empire, especially equipping and paying the huge army, took a toll on Rome. During the early years of expansion, the treasury grew as Roman troops conquered and plundered territories. As the Roman Empire weakened and no longer annexed new territories, it could no longer rely on plundered wealth. Yet the empire still needed to equip and maintain its army to maintain order. Without new plundered silver, the empire ran short on its main source of metal for currency. The government responded by decreasing the amount of silver in coins, leading to massive inflation. Diocletian's wage and price controls were only minimally effective in buttressing the economy for a short time. As farmers lost lands to invading forces, poverty and hunger increased. The people then lost faith in the Roman government to provide for their basic security.

Contribution of Political and Social Conflicts

Political upheaval and economic decline contributed to wide-scale social unrest and loss of faith in the Roman Empire. Reliance on slave labor had prevented Rome from developing a strong working or middle class. When small farmers lost land due to foreign invasions and the government proved unable to pay many of its soldiers, the people had to rely on charity just to survive. Yet the

Copyright © Mometrix Media. You have been licensed one copy of this document for personal use only. Any other reproduction or redistribution is strictly prohibited. All rights reserved.
This content is provided for test preparation purposes only and does not imply an endorsement by Mometrix of any particular political, scientific, or religious point of view.

government was unable to provide for the needs of an increasingly poor population. This situation fostered widespread resentment as the gap between rich and poor increased, and the public began to view its leaders as nothing more than corrupt, self-indulgent fools. Religious trends, such as increased conversion to Christianity and pagan religions, reflected loss of faith in the empire. The people turned increasingly to the church and themselves for survival. The centralized government had effectively dissolved by the time the last western Roman emperor, Romulus Augustus, was conquered by German forces in 476.

Copyright © Mometrix Media. You have been licensed one copy of this document for personal use only. Any other reproduction or redistribution is strictly prohibited. All rights reserved.
This content is provided for test preparation purposes only and does not imply an endorsement by Mometrix of any particular political, scientific, or religious point of view.

Early Modern Europe

Affects of Mapmaking and Navigation

The Crusades, expanded trade, and Renaissance examination of ancient writings led to an increased interest in mapmaking. Initially, global mapmakers relied on ancient, incomplete maps created by Ptolemy. Mapmakers sifted through more recent travel guides, as well as reports from explorations and military excursions, to create more accurate maps. These Renaissance-era maps still did not contain many places yet to be explored by Europeans (like the Americas), but they were much more complete than previous maps. Using the maps helped travelers reach far-off destinations in Africa and Asia. They also led some sailors to try to find faster, easier paths to distant markets, particularly a new path to Asia which would avoid traveling around Africa or through Arab-controlled waterways in the Middle East.

Along with improved maps, sailors sought inventions which would improve their ability to sail long distances while accurately reaching their destination. Improvements in the compass helped sailors identify their direction. The astrolabe helped them identify their position on the globe.

Improvement of Shipbuilding by the Portuguese and Spanish

Prior to 1500, most Europeans sailed in galleys, long cumbersome ships powered by oars with sails which relied upon favorable winds. Galleys were well-suited to coastlines, but not adequate for long excursions across the ocean. In the late 1400s, both Spain and Portugal began investing in ship improvements. They made their ships longer and larger, changed the size and shape of sails, and moved the rudder from the side to the rear of the ship. These modifications allowed the ships to sail against the wind, making sea travel faster, easier, and less dependent upon ideal weather conditions. Using new materials obtained through trade, the Portuguese and Spanish improved the durability and weather resistance of sails and rope, decreasing the chances of errors due to equipment failure.

Christopher Columbus

Christopher Columbus was an Italian navigator who, like many of his day, was looking for an easier route to Asia from Europe. After studying the works of Ptolemy, as well as the writings of Marco Polo, who visited Asia in the 1200s, Columbus came to believe that the shortest route would be to travel west from Europe. That part of the Atlantic was virtually unknown to contemporary Europeans (who knew nothing of the Viking explorations) and the subject of many frightening myths and legends. Columbus initially approached Portuguese King John II for financing, but he rejected the risky project. Finally after several fervent pleas, King Ferdinand and Queen Isabella, who were in the process of reinvigorating Spain, agreed to back the voyage. Columbus's three ships set sail in August of 1492 and landed in San Salvador on October 12.

Effects of Columbus's Voyages

Ferdinand and Isabella funded the voyage to gain wealth and new lands for settlement. When Columbus returned home from his first voyage to a hero's welcome, he brought back a little gold, some new spices, parrots, and Native Americans. He made three more journeys, exploring many of the Caribbean Islands, which he called the West Indies thinking they were in Asia, and parts of the coast off Central and South America. Columbus never found the source of Caribbean gold or any goods which held potential for large-scale trade, but his efforts did encourage colonization for agricultural development and further exploration. Columbus advocated for the large-scale enslavement of Native Americans, for the purpose of converting them to Christianity and "civilizing"

Copyright © Mometrix Media. You have been licensed one copy of this document for personal use only. Any other reproduction or redistribution is strictly prohibited. All rights reserved.
This content is provided for test preparation purposes only and does not imply an endorsement by Mometrix of any particular political, scientific, or religious point of view.

them. Isabella firmly opposed this plan, clashing openly with Columbus. By the time of his death in 1506, Columbus had fallen out of favor with the Crown, though they appreciated the new lands he had obtained for them. Columbus never believed he had found a new continent.

ACCOMPLISHMENTS OF NAVIGATORS AND EXPLORERS

- Amerigo Vespucci — Italian navigator who travelled with Atlantic expeditions between 1497 and 1504; one of the first navigators to recognize that the lands were part of a new continent, not Asia; in his honor, German mapmakers started labelling new lands "America"
- Vasco Núñez de Balboa — Spanish explorer who found link between Atlantic and Pacific Oceans when he crossed the Isthmus of Panama in 1513; called Pacific "the South Sea"
- Ferdinand Magellan — Portuguese navigator who led first expedition to circumnavigate the globe; found Balboa's South Sea by going around South America, called it the Pacific Ocean
- Ponce de León — Spaniard who explored Florida in 1513; searched for the Fountain of Youth
- John Cabot — Venetian who explored northern lands for England in 1497-98; claimed Newfoundland, Nova Scotia, and parts of New England
- Henry Hudson — Dutch explorer who sailed first for Netherlands, then for England: charted much of the land in what is now the northeastern United States and southern Canada

COMMERCIAL REVOLUTION

The opening of trade which helped spawn the Renaissance gradually spread beyond the Italian city-states and altered all the economies of Europe. During the medieval era, the manorial system had dominated the economies of most kingdoms. The expansion of trade and the wealth it brought encouraged more market-driven systems. Global trade and expanded markets required new economic systems beyond the scope of local manors or governments. National governments, wanting to encourage profitable ventures that would benefit the entire population, encouraged innovative new ideas in commerce and trade. What resulted was a radically new way of considering and managing economic activity.

AFFECTS OF LOCAL ECONOMIC SYSTEMS THE COMMERCIAL REVOLUTION

On the local level, as manors declined in importance, merchants and bankers took on a greater role. The use of coined money and scrip (usually in the form of I.O.U.s) became widespread, though barter continued to be common. Soon elements of capitalism evolved as business leaders looked for creative ways to raise capital for new projects. Bankers became more important as money lenders to support expansion and new business ventures, including some voyages of exploration. Merchants banded together to form joint-stock companies, which sold shares to stockholders. This system allowed the businesses to raise large sums of money while dispersing the risks among many people. The stockholders reaped the rewards if the company made a profit, offering incentives to those who owned more shares. If the company failed, the stockholders only lost their initial investment, while not being liable for any other company actions.

AFFECTS OF COMMERCIAL REVOLUTION ON NATIONAL ECONOMIES

The exchange of trade increased the need for standardized monetary systems. First city-states, then nations, began to issue their own unique money set at fixed rates of exchange. National economies were measured in the amount of silver and gold they owned. Trade, wars, and national pride led nations to compete with each another for dominance in the new global commercial economy. Each country strove for a favorable balance of trade, in some cases instituting tariffs to discourage the purchase of imports from certain rival countries. National economies also supported private

Copyright © Mometrix Media. You have been licensed one copy of this document for personal use only. Any other reproduction or redistribution is strictly prohibited. All rights reserved.
This content is provided for test preparation purposes only and does not imply an endorsement by Mometrix of any particular political, scientific, or religious point of view.

business endeavors, offering subsidies to businesses which enhanced national goals, and sponsoring scientific research and voyages of exploration.

PROMOTING COLONIZATION

Colonization supported the goals of rising nations. These goals included:

- Finding sources for raw materials needed by the European populations
- Finding items for trade that would appeal to foreign and domestic markets
- Obtaining raw silver and gold to support national treasuries and for the coinage of money
- Creating new markets for manufactured goods by the home country
- Providing a way to thin overpopulated regions by encouraging migration and resettlement
- Offering safe areas for religious and political dissenters to settle
- Encouraging the conversion of non-Christian populations in colonizing areas

TERMS

- Columbian Exchange —the exchange of goods between the Western and Eastern hemispheres following Columbus's voyages to the Americas
- triangular trade — system by which Europeans exchanged goods with the Americas; ships traveled first to Africa, trading European goods for slaves, who they hauled to the Americas; traders then sold slaves to plantation owners in exchange for American goods which were produced with slave labor
- Middle Passage — refers to the second stage of the triangular trade, when enslaved Africans were transported across the Atlantic to the Americas; notorious as a brutal voyage in which Africans, treated like commodities, were packed tightly into ships where disease festered and death was common
- mercantilism — system which came to dominate European economies; focused on nations owning large amounts of gold and silver ore which they used to fund all government projects

PORTUGAL'S AMERICAN EMPIRE

Portugal became an early leader in sea travel thanks largely to the efforts of Prince Henry, nicknamed "the Navigator." Henry had an ambitious plan to help his country master technologies of sea travel by supporting geographers and navigators. By the 1420s, he sponsored numerous voyages of exploration. Portugal dominated exploration throughout the 1400s, establishing strong trade ties with the East Indies. Portuguese explorers, like Bartolomeu Dias and Vasco da Gama, sought shorter routes to Asia. Recognizing the potential of Columbus's land discovery, Portugal competed with Spain for dominance in the Americas, leading the Treaty of Tordesillas, which divided unclaimed lands through an imaginary line in the ocean. Because of this treaty, Brazil became Portuguese while most of the rest of South America was Spanish. Portugal also continued claiming islands throughout the western Pacific. Unfortunately, Portugal did not have the funds, government structure, or manpower to sustain such a vast empire. By 1580, Portugal was so weak that Spain annexed it. Although public opposition led Portugal to reclaim its independence in 1640, it never again acted a major global force.

AFFECT OF CORTÉS AND PIZARRO

These two explorers were largely responsible for the Spanish conquest of Native Americans in Mexico and South America. Hernan Cortés led an invading force of conquistadors to Mexico in 1519. At that time, Mexico was dominated by the fierce Aztec nation led by Montezuma II. The Aztecs' oppressive treatment of other Native American groups made them widely feared and despised.

Copyright © Mometrix Media. You have been licensed one copy of this document for personal use only. Any other reproduction or redistribution is strictly prohibited. All rights reserved.
This content is provided for test preparation purposes only and does not imply an endorsement by Mometrix of any particular political, scientific, or religious point of view.

Cortés used this situation to his advantage, making alliances with groups which hated the Aztecs. The Spanish and their allies quickly conquered the Aztec forces, razing the city of Tenochtitlan (later, Mexico City). The defeat of the Aztec, coupled with a smallpox epidemic that decimated Native American groups, helped the Spanish maintain control of the region, which contained valuable sources of gold ore. In 1530, Francisco Pizarro led an expedition into South America, where the Spanish conquered the Inca of Peru and founded the city of Lima. This conquest gave the Spanish control of major silver mines which combined with gold sources further north to fund the Spanish government in Europe.

Dutch East India Company

The Dutch East India Company was founded in 1602 to organize and protect Dutch trading rights in the East Indies. The Netherlands' government granted the company exclusive rights to all Dutch sea trade between the Cape of Good Hope and the Straits of Magellan, but otherwise left the company alone to run itself. The well-organized company soon drove out the Portuguese and fended off the British. To support their endeavors, company leaders began to organize colonies, beginning with Java in 1619. They expanded trade into many regions where Europeans had never before traded, such as in Nagasaki, Japan. The company succeeded in part because it remained committed to its business purpose of making a profit, unlike other traders who wanted to convert or change the cultures of native populations. The company's successful Asian trade allowed it to fund voyages of exploration and colonization in other regions, including the Americas. In 1626, it purchased the island of Manhattan from Native Americans for the establishment of New Amsterdam (New York City).

Britain's Role in Sea Trade

Britain was late to rise as a sea power, but quickly caught up with and surpassed its rivals. Although John Cabot claimed North American lands for the British in the 1490s, the British government was too unstable to focus attention on colonization or exploration until the reign of Elizabeth I. While military leaders worked to modernize the navy, Elizabeth dispatched a group of pirates called the seadogs to undermine Spanish and Portuguese trade. These men, led by John Hawkins, Francis Drake, and Walter Raleigh, attacked seafaring vessels, plundering the wealth of England's enemies. Elizabeth publicly claimed the seadogs were renegades over whom she had no control. Meanwhile, she authorized creation of the British East India Company to expand trade ties. Initially the company made no effort to colonize, focusing mainly on establishing diplomatic relations that allowed for the building of trading posts in Asian markets, undermining rival nations.

British Monarchy and Parliament

Members of Parliament considered themselves to be the voice of the people, entrusted to protect them against abuses by the monarchy. At this time Parliament's House of Lords was made up mainly of nobles and clergy. The House of Commons represented the gentry (landowners) and burgesses (businessmen). Recognizing their importance as representatives of the people, Elizabeth I worked closely and usually successfully with Parliament. During this era, however, Parliament only met when convened by the monarch, thus Elizabeth rarely called the body into session and usually only when she needed to raise taxes (which it usually approved). James I, who lacked Elizabeth's political savvy and promoted absolute monarchy, clashed openly with Parliament over his desire for greater control of the government. Parliament reacted by denying his requests to raise taxes. James also faced opposition from Puritan members of Parliament who wanted the government to reform the Anglican Church. As a result, James's reign created more divisions between the legislature and monarchy.

Copyright © Mometrix Media. You have been licensed one copy of this document for personal use only. Any other reproduction or redistribution is strictly prohibited. All rights reserved.
This content is provided for test preparation purposes only and does not imply an endorsement by Mometrix of any particular political, scientific, or religious point of view.

Division of the Kingdom of Charles V

Charles, a member of the Habsburg family, became king of Spain in 1516 and Holy Roman Emperor and Archduke of Austria in 1519. His kingdom, consisting of numerous and often conflicting ethnicities and interests, proved too vast to manage as he faced problems on all fronts. Wars between Catholics and Protestants drained resources and manpower. Spain faced food shortages because of overdependence on wool production, as well as war with France. In the east, Charles's troops faced invading Turks. Charles even found himself at odds with the pope, leading his troops to sack Rome in 1527. After years of constant fighting, Charles came to believe that no one king could lead such a vast area. In 1556, he retired and split his kingdom. Charles V's son, Philip II, became king of Spain and the Netherlands. Charles named his brother Ferdinand (already king of Hungary and Bohemia) as Holy Roman Emperor and king of Austria.

Philip II of Spain

Unlike many Spanish monarchs, Philip was born and raised in Spain with strong feelings of national pride. An ardent Catholic, Philip strove to protect his nation from Protestant incursions and built it into a dominant European power. He built a lavish royal palace in Madrid, from which he ruled an absolute monarchy. Philip insisted on approving all edicts, appointments, and patronages. Although all government business throughout the empire was supposed to go through him, Philip rarely left his castle and never left the Iberian Peninsula after 1559. Although a hardworking king, Philip's isolation cut him off from his subjects and made him increasingly paranoid. His suspicions of even his closest advisors spawned infighting within the royal court which permeated into the provinces. Adding to the spirit of mistrust, Philip sanctioned abusive tactics by the Inquisition to suppress heresy. For many years Philip avoided foreign wars, but his worries about Protestantism led him into battles with England and France, who both supported a popular anti-Spanish uprising in the Netherlands.

Netherlands' Rebellion Against Spain

The Netherlands originated as the Dutch-speaking lowland provinces of the Habsburg Empire. Sitting inland, but below sea level, this dike-protected region survived as a successful, rather independent trading center. During the Protestant Reformation many Dutch speakers converted to Calvinism. When Charles V split his empire he gave Philip control of the Netherlands. Almost immediately Philip tried to impose his will on the region, usurping the traditional power of local nobles. He taxed the Dutch more heavily than the Spanish and persecuted Calvinists. All of these policies angered the Dutch and fostered resentment against Philip, which soon broke out into full-scale revolt. In 1568, William of Orange led an attack on Spanish forces using guerrilla warfare and tactics such as opening dikes to flood the enemy. In 1579, the northern Netherlands declared their independence, though Philip refused to recognize it. Fighting continued even after William of Orange was killed in 1584. The northern Netherlands did not gain their independence until the Treaty of Westphalia in 1648. The lower provinces remained the Spanish Netherlands.

Conflicts Between England and Spain

The major conflicts between England and Spain were influenced by religion and the personalities of the countries' leaders. The conflicts arose from Henry VIII's break with the Catholic Church and creation of the Church of England. This move angered leaders in Catholic Spain, who determined to defend their faith against rising Protestantism. One of their main goals was to destroy the Anglican Church and restore English Catholicism. England's Catholic queen, Mary I, wed Spain's Catholic king, Philip II. He later conspired with Mary Queen of Scots to assassinate Elizabeth I, leading to Mary's execution. Such efforts only served to anger Elizabeth and her supporters, who not only determined to protect the Anglican faith, but to weaken rival Spain. To that end, England began

Copyright © Mometrix Media. You have been licensed one copy of this document for personal use only. Any other reproduction or redistribution is strictly prohibited. All rights reserved.
This content is provided for test preparation purposes only and does not imply an endorsement by Mometrix of any particular political, scientific, or religious point of view.

supporting Dutch efforts against the Spanish. English expansion of trade and the efforts of the seadogs further angered Philip, as did Elizabeth's denials of involvement in the piracy. The personal animosity which developed between Elizabeth and Philip reflected English fears that Spain's wealth would allow it to dominate Europe and eventually absorb England.

Spanish Armada

Angered by his conflicts with Elizabeth, Spain's king Philip II determined to directly attack England. He organized 30,000 soldiers and sailors into the 130-ship Spanish Armada. The fleet attacked across the Straits of Dover in July 1588. The Spanish ships were mainly large transports, designed to carry huge numbers of soldiers and get them within range of other vessels to attack and board via small craft. The English had fewer ships, most of which were small vessels that relied on heavy, long-range artillery. In essence, the two fleets were prepared to fight very different types of battles. The English strategy proved superior for the straits, where their quick, maneuverable ships harassed and thwarted the Spanish. Soon joined by Dutch vessels, the English launched an attack to separate the Armada. The plan worked, leaving individual ships vulnerable to attack. After experiencing heavy damage and high casualties for days, the Armada retreated with less than half its fleet. The Spanish ships which survived were severely damaged. The defeat saved England and the Netherlands, signaled the decline of Spain, and ushered in a new era of seafaring combat.

Decline of Spain's power

The defeat of the Spanish Armada marked a huge blow to Spain on many levels. The destruction of the navy left Spain's coasts and trading vessels less secure. More importantly, it emboldened Spain's enemies and weakened Spanish confidence in their own leaders. Philip's wars in defense of Catholicism proved to be costly in both money and manpower. In addition to the failed effort against England, he also launched a failed invasion of France to stop the spread of Protestantism there. Spain also failed to modernize its economy because it was slow to develop a middle class or manufacturing, instead holding on to traditional class systems. The Reconquista had driven out many of Spain's most talented Jewish and Muslim innovators. The wealthy used gold and silver obtained from the Americas to buy goods produced in other countries, leading to a trade deficit. Eventually, these factors would undermine public faith in the government and lead Spain to fall behind other European powers.

Thirty Years' War

The war was actually a series of conflicts that began in 1618 and lasted until 1648. The conflict initially began as a dispute over religion, but evolved into a power grab by various countries to win control of the unorganized German kingdoms. Fighting originated in Bohemia and Austria when the king and future Holy Roman Emperor tried to suppress non-Catholics. Protestants rose up in rebellion. Through they lost this initial war, other powers intervened to keep the fighting going, most hoping to emerge with control of lands for themselves. Sweden's Protestant leader attacked pro-Catholic German kingdoms. Poland invaded neighboring Russia, then Sweden. Under the direction of Cardinal Richelieu, France instigated much of the fighting, while avoiding direct combat itself. The wars finally ended with the multi-nation Treaty of Westphalia, which declared several new nations in Eastern Europe, strengthened the influence of France, and further weakened the influence of Spain.

Long Parliament

After Charles I, a believer in absolute monarchy, became king in 1625, Parliament refused to approve any new taxes he requested. When Charles tried to seize private property without approval, Parliament presented him with the Petition of Right, limiting his power. Though Charles signed the document under pressure, he then dismissed Parliament and blatantly violated the

Copyright © Mometrix Media. You have been licensed one copy of this document for personal use only. Any other reproduction or redistribution is strictly prohibited. All rights reserved.
This content is provided for test preparation purposes only and does not imply an endorsement by Mometrix of any particular political, scientific, or religious point of view.

agreement. Charles refused to convene Parliament for 11 years, during which time he further angered the public by oppressing Puritanism and Presbyterianism, a growing Scottish sect. The Scots launched a rebellion, which Charles was unable to put down. Realizing he needed Parliament's help to fund the war, he finally called it into session in 1640. When Parliament refused to approve new taxes, Charles dissolved it again. The Scots responded by attacking England. Charles reluctantly called Parliament into session. This time, it not only turned down his tax appeal, but passed new laws limiting the monarch's power, including the power to convene and dissolve Parliament. This Long Parliament met off and on for years, constantly struggling against Charles.

English Civil War

During the Long Parliament, England faced a rebellion in Ireland, compounding the revolt it already faced in Scotland. Now even Parliament recognized the need to fund a larger army, but its leaders did not trust Charles. The leaders proposed that Parliament be in charge of armies instead of the king. In 1642, Charles led troops to arrest five leaders of the House of Commons. Over the next several months his supporters, the nobility-led Cavaliers, and Parliament's supporters, the Puritan-backed Roundheads, began preparing for civil war. Fighting began at the Battle of Edgehill in October 1642. Scottish support helped the Roundheads defeat the Cavaliers by May of 1646. Charles tried to flee and organize a rally, but failed. He was captured, tried for treason, and executed. Parliament abolished the monarchy and the nobility-led House of Lords, declaring England a commonwealth. Although both the monarchy and House of Lords would later be restored, parliamentary dominance in England was firmly established.

Oliver Cromwell

Oliver Cromwell was an English politician who joined the Puritan movement as an adult. He became a member of the House of Commons in 1528, not long before Parliament presented Charles with the Petition of Right. Cromwell became a vocal opponent of the king, largely because of Charles's oppression of Puritans. When the English Civil War broke out, Cromwell proved his skills as a military leader, organizing the New Model Army, made up of 11 cavalry regiments of 600 men each; 12 foot infantry regiments, made up of 1,200 men each; and 1,000 mounted infantry called dragoons. This massive force was able to defeat Charles's troops. Cromwell's leadership both in Parliament and on the battlefield during the crisis helped him assume leadership of the country following the execution of Charles.

Scientific Revolution

The Scientific Revolution grew out of humanism and the general spirit of the Renaissance. The new focus on education, reason, and questioning of authority led many learned individuals to question accepted notions of the natural world, many of which were based on tradition, theology, and superstition. As students of classical education studied ancient Greek and Roman writings, they examined early scientific thought, especially that which originated with the Greeks. This research led many students to develop their own scientific theories, as well as the scientific method of experimentation to test theories, often resulting in new inventions. The new methods were based on human observation using the senses and reason. As scientific research grew, it began to radically challenge the way people perceived the world around them and soon changed the way in which people lived.

Copyright © Mometrix Media. You have been licensed one copy of this document for personal use only. Any other reproduction or redistribution is strictly prohibited. All rights reserved.
This content is provided for test preparation purposes only and does not imply an endorsement by Mometrix of any particular political, scientific, or religious point of view.

Contributions of Copernicus, Kepler, and Galileo

All of the men were scientists who challenged traditional thought about planetary motion.

- Nicolaus Copernicus — Astronomer who challenged Ptolemy's geocentric view of the universe; published *Six Books Concerning the Revolutions of the Heavenly Orbs* in 1543, advocating for a heliocentric theory, but could not test his theories
- Kepler — Mathematician who tried to prove Copernicus's theory using models and mathematical equations; developed what became known as three laws of planetary motion; published *New Astronomy* in 1609
- Galileo Galilei — Astronomer who built telescope; observations helped prove Copernicus's theory; also challenged Aristotle's theory that heavy objects fell faster than light by saying that all objects fall at same rate; published *Dialogue Concerning the Two Chief World Systems, Ptolemaic & Copernican* in 1632; faced rebuke from Inquisition

Contributions of Roger Bacon, Rene Descartes, and Francis Bacon.

All contributed to the development of scientific methodology.

- Roger Bacon — English philosopher, monk, and scientist from the 1200s who preceded the Renaissance, but whose ideas influenced those who led the Scientific Revolution; advocated for scientific experimentation
- Descartes — Multi-disciplined French thinker who in early 1600s advocated reliance upon provable facts; wrote *Discourse on Methods* to promote ideas; quote "I think, therefore I am"; Descartes' challenge to Catholic thought led to his banishment in Protestant Sweden
- Francis Bacon — English philosopher who promoted testing of "facts" by physical observation, rather than reason alone; promoted system of experimentation, described in *Novum Organum* (1620).

Contributions of Vesalius, Harvey, and Paré.

All made major advances in medical sciences.

- Andreas Vesalius — Flemish scientist who made great advances in study of anatomy which were based on his personal examinations and observations; heavily illustrated textbook *On the Fabric of the Human Body* (1543) changed the way people viewed human anatomy
- William Harvey — English doctor in early 1600s who advanced understanding of the circulatory system through laboratory experiments; first to accurately explain how blood cycles through veins, arteries, and heart
- Ambroise Paré — French doctor; considered father of modern surgery; experience as military surgeon in wars of the 1500s helped make advances in surgical techniques; developed use of stitches to close wounds

Puritans

Puritans were religious reformers who sought to cleanse or purify (hence the name) the Anglican Church of its remaining vestiges of Roman Catholic traditions and ceremony. Puritans believed in living and working in a simple manner. Their theology stressed the need for individuals to be in a covenant relationship with God, manifest through the Holy Spirit. They placed a great deal of importance on preaching. Although emerging out of Anglicanism, the Puritans were heavily influenced by Calvinism. They believed in predestination of the elect and in building communities committed to rigid, moral living. Although originally a sect of Anglicanism, the Puritans eventually broke away and formed new denominations.

Copyright © Mometrix Media. You have been licensed one copy of this document for personal use only. Any other reproduction or redistribution is strictly prohibited. All rights reserved.
This content is provided for test preparation purposes only and does not imply an endorsement by Mometrix of any particular political, scientific, or religious point of view.

Jamestown vs. Plymouth

Jamestown, the first permanent English settlement in North America, was launched by the Virginia Company as a business venture. The colonists who arrived in the spring of 1607 were mainly soldiers whose job was to secure the area and establish a stable money-making settlement. As more colonists arrived, the settlement remained unstable and somewhat lawless, facing hardships and starvation until the cultivation of cash crop tobacco in 1614. Colonists who later came to Jamestown were primarily looking to gain money or land. Many indentured servants migrated until the large-scale importation of slaves changed the workforce.

The Plymouth colony was settled for religious freedom. Many of the colonists who settled there in 1620 were Pilgrims, members of the English Separatist Church, a radical sect of Puritanism. They envisioned building the perfect Separatist society, a "city on a hill" that would be a beacon of righteous living for the world. As a result, Plymouth was from the beginning much more stable, community-oriented, and rigid in its legal system.

European Life in the 1500s

In many ways, the culture of common folk remained similar to that of the medieval era, with some refinement as people were exposed to arts and new inventions. The vast majority of Europeans worked in agriculture and lived in simple, thatched-roof houses. Everything revolved around the crops and seasons. Life expectancy was short, and violence was common. The Commercial Revolution brought about new opportunities for many people. Skilled jobs grew in availability. Many people moved from farms to cities to earn wages. Later, many people migrated to the colonies in search of new opportunities. Improved crop production and imports from colonies decreased hunger. Although the majority of people were still illiterate, their exposure to printed words increased. Even small villages received broadsides which kept them informed about news. Some people came to depend on almanacs to help them predict the weather or other future events. In some regions, the decline of the Catholic Church ushered in new, non-Catholic traditions and customs. The greatest change was the idea that people could take advantage of new opportunities to change their destinies.

Influence of European Diets on the Expansion of Trade

Until the Commercial Revolution, Europeans ate strictly for survival, and it was generally not an enjoyable experience. European food throughout the Middle Ages tended to be very dull and bland in taste, comprised mainly of grain foods such as porridges and breads. Protein came mainly in the form of cheeses or eggs. Meat and fish were rare treats. Due to poor preservation methods, food spoiled easily, making it even less appealing and less healthy. The main preservative, salt, was too expensive for most common peasants to obtain. The opening of trade introduced new foods and especially spices which livened the taste of European dishes. As trade became easier, these imports became cheaper, allowing even lower wage earners to afford them. Salt and other preservatives also became more affordable. Colonization introduced Europeans to a variety of new plant foods, some of which they learned to also grow in Europe. "Luxury" food items such as tea, coffee, chocolate, and sugar changed the European palette, ushering in new attitudes towards eating and drinking.

Copyright © Mometrix Media. You have been licensed one copy of this document for personal use only. Any other reproduction or redistribution is strictly prohibited. All rights reserved.
This content is provided for test preparation purposes only and does not imply an endorsement by Mometrix of any particular political, scientific, or religious point of view.

Medieval History

Justinian Code

In the A.D. 500s, after the fall of the Roman Empire, Byzantine emperor Justinian ordered the creation of this four-part codex as a way of preserving the ancient Roman legal system. Most importantly, he wanted to preserve the idea that laws, rather than individual leaders, should form the basis of government. Byzantine scholars worked for many years to collect and document Roman laws and legal thought. The Justinian Code eventually included laws created under the old Roman Empire, Roman legal opinions, a textbook for students of the law, and new regulations added by the Byzantines. The Justinian Code not only became the basis for the Byzantine legal system, but also served as the model for most western European nations. It is primarily because of the Justinian Code that Roman legal thought survived to become the basis for western constitutional law.

Byzantine Empire

The Byzantine Empire's strengths were most evident during its early reign. Its weaknesses began to emerge during its later period.

Strengths:

- Strong imperial system under wise leaders
- Well-organized, centralized bureaucracy that maintained order
- Skilled diplomats who forged foreign alliances, often through arranged marriages
- Skilled army with advanced weaponry
- Skilled navy that perfected techniques such as the use of combustible chemicals, such as "Greek fire"
- Strategic location of Constantinople along trade routes
- Fair taxation system which brought wealth to the empire

Weaknesses:

- Ineffective later kings
- Inability to adapt to modern commerce
- Ethnic conflict
- Inability to maintain order as geographic boundaries expanded
- Loss of support from western allies
- Inability to compete against stronger Turkish armies

Importance of Ostrogoths, Visigoths, Lombards, Slavs, Bulgars, and Avars

They were all barbaric tribes which rose to power in Europe after the fall of the Western Roman Empire.

- Ostrogoths — Arose in the Baltic Sea and invaded Italian Peninsula in 400s; under Theodoric the Great, established kingdom of Italy in 493; defeated by Justinian in the mid-550s; also called "Goths"
- Visigoths — Split from the Ostrogoths in the 300s; converted to Arian Christianity; established kingdoms in Spain and Gaul in 400s; also called "Goths"
- Lombards — Originated in Pannonia region of modern Hungary; under King Alboin, invaded Italy in 568 and established several independent kingdoms

Copyright © Mometrix Media. You have been licensed one copy of this document for personal use only. Any other reproduction or redistribution is strictly prohibited. All rights reserved.
This content is provided for test preparation purposes only and does not imply an endorsement by Mometrix of any particular political, scientific, or religious point of view.

- Slavs — Arose in the late 500s to take control of most of the Balkan Peninsula by 602.
- Avars — Arose in the mid-500s to take control of the region between the Adriatic and Balkan Seas; often allied with other tribes
- Bulgars — Originated in central Asia or Turkey; fought first for the Huns, then the Byzantines; defeated by Avars; unified under Kurt, who established kingdom around Sea of Azov

Nika Revolt

By the early 500s, Byzantine society had developed various associations, or demes, that represented different political and social factions. To avoid real civil war between the groups, Byzantine leaders encouraged them to challenge one another in sporting events. By 532, tensions were high among the two strongest associations, the Blue and the Green, when they met to compete at the Hippodrome in Constantinople. A riot broke out that lasted for days, killing thousands and destroying much of the city. "Nika," meaning "win" or "conquer" was a slogan shouted by the rebels. Justinian's political opponents tried to use the unrest to stage a coup. Justinian considered fleeing, but was convinced by Queen Theodora to stay and defend his crown. Under the leadership of generals Belisarius and Mundus, Justinian's army put down the rebellion and ended the political opposition. Justinian emerged stronger than ever before.

Iconoclastic Controversy

By the late 600s, many Christians had adopted the use of icons, or holy images of Jesus, the Virgin Mary, or saints of the church. Many people seemed to almost worship the icons more than God. Other Christians, called iconoclasts, opposed the use of icons, arguing that they violated the second of the Ten Commandments. In 726, Byzantine emperor and iconoclast Leo III outlawed the use of icons. Some church leaders argued that the use of icons helped spread the Christian message to the majority of Europeans, who could neither read nor write. In 787, the Council of Nicaea, with support from Pope Adrian I, ruled iconoclastism to be heresy. While then-Byzantine empress Irene re-instated the use of icons, many Christian leaders, especially in the east, continued to oppose their use. The conflict eventually contributed to the 1054 split of the Christian church into the western-based Roman Catholic Church and the Eastern Orthodox Church. Despite remaining split, the Eastern Orthodox Church eventually came to accept the use of icons.

Byzantine culture terms

All are terms associated with Byzantine culture.

- Cyrillic alphabet — Alphabet believed to have been invented in the A.D. 800s or 900s by Eastern Orthodox missionaries Cyril and Methodius; created for Slavs living in the Byzantine Empire, who had no prior written language; influenced by Greek alphabet, but with additional letters to reflect greater diversity of sounds in Slavic languages; basis for several Eastern European alphabets, including Russian
- Mosaic — type of artwork in which a picture is created using broken bits of glass, metal, or stone; perfected in the Byzantine Empire, especially in religious architecture; differed from western religious art in that it intentionally tried to create unrealistic, more spiritual, reflections of holy images
- Hagia Sophia — huge cathedral built in Constantinople; completed in A.D. 537, represents the greatest example of Byzantine art and architecture; first structure with a round dome topping a rectangular building
- Gynaeceum — section of the Hagia Sophia reserved for women; reflected gender segregation typical of the culture

Copyright © Mometrix Media. You have been licensed one copy of this document for personal use only. Any other reproduction or redistribution is strictly prohibited. All rights reserved.
This content is provided for test preparation purposes only and does not imply an endorsement by Mometrix of any particular political, scientific, or religious point of view.

Decline of the Byzantine Empire

After Justinian's death in A.D. 565, the empire went through a series of weak leaders. At the same time, invading groups including the Persians, the barbaric tribes, and Arabic Muslims began to seize control of outer portions of the empire. The empire experienced a resurgence under the Macedonian dynasty founded by Basil in 867. When the Seljuk Turks invaded in the 1000s, the Byzantines had to seek help from western forces to protect Constantinople. While this alliance helped save the empire temporarily, it also revealed its weaknesses. During the Crusades of the 1200s, western forces tried to retake control of Constantinople. The city's location made it a much sought-after prize in the Christian-Muslim conflicts. The further-weakened Byzantines retook control of the city in 1261, but soon the Ottoman Turks were invading the empire. The Byzantine Empire finally collapsed when the Ottomans seized Constantinople in 1453.

Islam

Life of Muhammad and the Founding of the Islamic Faith

- c. A.D. 570 Muhammad was born in Mecca.
- 610 Muhammad reported a vision in which the Angel Gabriel appeared to him and began revealing prophecies and teachings that would become the basis for the holy text of Islam, the Qur'an.
- 610-622 As Muhammad's teachings spread, he angered members of his own tribe, the Quraysh, by denouncing their traditional religion based on animism.
- 622 Muhammad officially declared that there was only one God, the same god of Abraham. The announcement so angered members of the Quraysh that they plotted to kill him.
- 622 Muhammad completed the hijrah, or "migration," to Yathrib from Mecca. Yathrib was renamed Medina, for "City of the Prophet." It became the center of the early Islamic faith.
- 624 The Battle of Badr marked the beginning of war between Mecca and Medina over the Islamic faith.
- 630 Mecca surrendered to Muhammad, who declared it a Muslim city.
- 632 Muhammad died in Medina.

Five Pillars of Islam

The Five Pillars are five basic acts of worship required of all faithful Muslims. They include:

- shahadah - Profession of faith, "There is no god but Allah; Muhammad is the prophet of Allah."
- salat – Ritual of five daily prayers, recited in the morning, noon, afternoon, at sunset, and nighttime; ideally facing towards Muhammad's birthplace of Mecca.
- zakat – Payments made to provide for the poor and needy within a community, amount based on one's material wealth.
- sawm – Period of fasting during the holy month of Ramadan, when Muslims are supposed to focus on obedience to the Qur'an.
- hajj – Pilgrimage to holy city of Mecca which should be completed at least once during one's lifetime if one is able.

Developments in the Islamic Empire

After Muhammad's death, his followers chose his closest advisor, Abu Bakr, to lead the faith. Under Abu Bakr, Islamic forces sought to secure control of the Arabian Peninsula and began to expand outward into what is now Syria and Iran. After Abu Bakr died, Umar I, another trusted advisor, took control. Under Umar, the Islamic Empire spread into the Persian Empire and what is now Iraq. He set forth many of the policies that later rulers would follow to control these conquered lands.

Copyright © Mometrix Media. You have been licensed one copy of this document for personal use only. Any other reproduction or redistribution is strictly prohibited. All rights reserved.
This content is provided for test preparation purposes only and does not imply an endorsement by Mometrix of any particular political, scientific, or religious point of view.

Further leaders continued expansion by conquest or treaty, benefiting from the weakening of other powers such as the Byzantines. In 710, the Moors led by Tariq expanded Islam into Spain, establishing a foothold in Europe. By the 900s, large numbers of the warring Turkish clans had converted to Islam. Turkish Muslims came to dominate much of the Islamic Empire, expanding into northern India by the early 1200s. The Turks established more secular systems of government than the Arabic Muslims.

Differences between the Sunni, Shiite, and Sufi Faiths

After the death of Umar I, his successor, Uthman, was assassinated by rebels who claimed he favored members of his own clan. Uthman's relatives, including Mu'awiyah, opposed the new caliph, Ali, accusing him of having been part of the assassination plot. Civil war broke out between the two sides, with Mu'awiyah emerging as the victorious caliph in A.D. 661. Many Muslims continued to believe that Ali's descendants should lead the faith. They became known as Shiites. Supporters of Mu'awiyah became known as Sunnis, from the word "Sunna" ("Way of the Prophet"). Theologically, the two differed over leadership in religious and secular affairs. Sunnis believed that common followers should discuss and resolve religious disputes, maintaining separation of spiritual and secular affairs. Shiites believed that imams should be vested with power over both religious and secular affairs. Sufism emerged around 800 as a mystic movement within Islam. Sufis were ascetics who rejected the imperial goals of the Islamic Empire. Sufism eventually emerged as a distinct faith from Islam.

Terms

- caliph – Title meaning "successor of the Prophet"; used to refer to main leaders of the Islamic faith following Mohammad's death
- imam – Religious and secular leaders among Shiite Muslims; descendents of defeated caliph Ali
- sultan – Government leader among Turkish Muslims; answered to the caliph, but held power over secular, not spiritual, issues
- sheik – Leader of an Arabic tribe; traditionally a title of respect for any elderly or respected man in Arabic society
- vizier – Government officials who carried out the orders of sultans in the Turkish Islamic Empire

Arab Contributions to Science and Mathematics

- Advanced study and improvements upon Greek studies in math and science
- Physician al-Razi's collections of medical knowledge
- Ibn Sina's *Canon of Medicine,* textbook widely studied by medical students for centuries
- Al-Idrisi's improved maps of the world, made for the court of Sicily
- Improved astrolabe, which allowed sailors to chart their position on Earth in relation to the stars
- Development of the Arabic number system, which became the basis for the western system of commerce and measurement
- Expanded use of decimals
- Development of algebra
- Advances in trigonometry

Copyright © Mometrix Media. You have been licensed one copy of this document for personal use only. Any other reproduction or redistribution is strictly prohibited. All rights reserved.
This content is provided for test preparation purposes only and does not imply an endorsement by Mometrix of any particular political, scientific, or religious point of view.

Contributions to the Arts and Literature

- Calligraphy - the art of fine handwriting, incorporated even on Islamic architecture
- Mosque architecture - because Islamic law forbade representations of the human form, mosques did not contain images of religious or spiritual leaders like Christian churches did; mosques focused much more on elaborate geometrical designs; most contained a minaret, or tower, from which a crier would call followers to their daily prayers; among the most spectacular buildings was the mosque at Cordoba, completed in 988.
- Literature - *The Thousand and One Nights,* a compilation of folktales allegedly told by the doomed bride Scheherazade, to delay her execution; includes characters such as Aladdin, Sinbad, and Ali Baba.

The Dark Ages

This term primarily refers to the early Middle Ages between A.D. 500 and 1000, after the fall of the western Roman Empire gave rise to a chaotic period marked by wars and uncertainty. The term once referred to the retreat of civilized behavior and knowledge that followed the end of Roman dominance, though this image has been somewhat exaggerated. This period did witness a decentralization of power and fragmentation of societies that had been connected to one another under Roman rule. During the Dark Ages, much of Europe retreated into a more isolated existence without dependable trade routes to connect to other cultures. Knowledge about other peoples most certainly declined during this period.

Franks

As the Roman Empire weakened, much of Europe fell into chaos. Warring tribes controlled small kingdoms and often fought with one another. The Franks, made up of several German-speaking tribes originally near the Rhine River, emerged as one of the more powerful of these groups. Under the ruler Clovis I, the Franks had conquered all of Gaul by the time the Western Roman Empire fully collapsed. Because Clovis had converted to Christianity, the emerging church embraced and supported his rule. In the 700s, Frankish leader Charles Martel defeated the Spanish Moors, thus halting the spread of Islamic rule in Europe. His son, Pepin III (also called Pepin the Short), formed a strong alliance with the Catholic Church. After repelling an attempted German invasion of Italy, Pepin gave the pope the lands that would become the Papal States. This gift strengthened the mutual political power of both the Frankish rulers and the Catholic Church.

Merovingians and Carolingians

Both families created lines of rulers for the Franks. The Merovingians were descended from Clovis I, who came to power in A.D. 481. They were so-called because Clovis traced his ancestry back to a man name Merovech. Clovis absorbed many of the Frankish tribes. The Merovingians included Pepin II, who unified all the Frankish tribes, and Charles Martel, who halted the Muslim advance in Spain. Pepin III overthrew the last Merovingian king to establish the Carolingian line of rulers. This line had the strong blessing of the pope. Pepin's son, Charlemagne, became the strongest of all the Frankish rulers. After his death in 814, later Carolingian rulers proved weak and unable to get along. In 843, they divided Charlemagne's empire into three smaller kingdoms. Lacking respect for their weak kings, many nobles began to rebel against the monarchy and seize power for themselves. Invasions from barbarian groups such as the Magyars and Vikings finally led to the collapse of the Carolingian monarchy, which was replaced by small feudalistic kingdoms.

Copyright © Mometrix Media. You have been licensed one copy of this document for personal use only. Any other reproduction or redistribution is strictly prohibited. All rights reserved.
This content is provided for test preparation purposes only and does not imply an endorsement by Mometrix of any particular political, scientific, or religious point of view.

CHARLEMAGNE

Charlemagne's major accomplishment's included:

- ruling the Frankish kingdom from 768 to 814
- conquering warring tribes to secure Frankish control over central and western Europe
- defeating the Lombards in Italy
- defeating the Saxons in Northern Europe
- defeating the Avars in central Europe
- driving the Moors back across the Pyrenees Mountains to establish a buffer zone between Christian and Muslim lands
- firmly establishing France and Germany as the center of power on the continent
- reviving Roman law and governmental practices
- strengthening and spreading the Christian faith among the conquered peoples
- increasing the power of the Catholic Church
- through his coronation by Pope Leo III, establishing the position of Holy Roman Emperor over Europe
- establishing a system of government led by counts, dukes, and the *missi dominici* to maintain order and enforce policies throughout the empire
- encouraging education by establishing schools for young nobles and many libraries throughout Europe

DEVELOPMENT OF FEUDALISM

Feudalism was a system of government and military defense. After the fall of the Carolingian monarchy, Europe devolved into an unorganized land of scattered, tiny kingdoms. Without a centralized government, Europeans needed a way to protect themselves from invading forces as well as from greedy neighboring kingdoms. To ensure loyalty and defense, kings would grant segments of land to nobles for their complete control. In return, the nobles had to swear loyalty and military defense to the king. Nobles in turn distributed smaller segments of land to vassals to protect and cultivate. Serfs worked the land in exchange for food, clothing, shelter, and protection. Nobles also organized armies of knights, who received protection and living needs in exchange for their defense of the land. All levels of the feudalistic system relied upon the exchange of goods for loyalty and defense. Even lands owned by the Catholic Church were managed through a feudalistic structure.

TERMS

- lord – under the medieval European system of feudalism, a noble who controlled land in a specific geographic region
- fief – under the system of feudalism, a section of land a lord granted to another to control and protect
- vassal – under the system of feudalism, a person who received a fief from a lord; often a lesser noble who might divide the land further and grant smaller fiefs to others
- homage – under the system of feudalism, an oath that a vassal took promising loyalty to the lord who granted the fief
- primogeniture – system of inheritance in which the eldest son received full control over all family assets upon the death of the father; widely practiced under the feudalistic system

MANORIAL SYSTEM

Manorialism was an economic structure that developed under the political system of feudalism as a way of maintaining and producing wealth for kingdoms and/or the church. The lord of the manor

Copyright © Mometrix Media. You have been licensed one copy of this document for personal use only. Any other reproduction or redistribution is strictly prohibited. All rights reserved.
This content is provided for test preparation purposes only and does not imply an endorsement by Mometrix of any particular political, scientific, or religious point of view.

subdivided the land to peasants, also called serfs, to cultivate. The serfs were usually allowed to keep just enough of the crop to support themselves, while the rest was turned over to the lord's control. All members of peasant families, including young children, worked. Peasants often lived in row houses arranged closely together for safety. Jobs other than farming were assigned by the lord for the benefit of the manor as a whole. Many non-agricultural jobs, such as knights, were reserved only for nobles. Lords, knights, and other nobility lived in a castle complex on the manor, supported by the extra goods they obtained from the peasants in exchange for protection.

LIFE FOR WOMEN ON MANORS

Life for peasant women was often harsh, as it was for most serfs. They worked long days at hard labor for which they saw very little reward. Because children were valuable as laborers, peasant women often gave birth many times, under conditions that were often life-threatening. Life expectancy for these women was very short. Noblewomen often assisted their husbands in some of their duties. Noblewomen were also expected to oversee the domestic workings of the manor. Education for noblewomen consisted mainly of training in domestic arts and manners. Marriages were often arranged, with landholdings exchanged as part of the noblewoman's dowry.

FEUDALISM AND MANORIALISM

Strengths — The two systems provided stability during uncertain times. They provided a framework for economic development and defense that worked in a land composed of small kingdoms with threats from outside forces.

Weaknesses — The quality of life under feudalism and manorialism often varied depending on the quality of the leadership provided by the nobles. They also locked people into a rigid class system in which there was virtually no opportunity for advancement. A peasant could never aspire to become a noble, for example. The economy was overly dependent upon agriculture, with very little knowledge or goods acquired through trade. There was little room for change or adaptation within the systems.

HIERARCHY OF THE CATHOLIC CHURCH

- At the lowest level was the parish priest, who served to a small geographic area and administered the sacraments to ordinary people.
- Several parishes made up a diocese, headed by a bishop. The bishop appointed and oversaw the work of the priests.
- Several dioceses made up an archdiocese, headed by an archbishop.
- Some archbishops were chosen to serve on the curia, a group that advised the pope.
- The pope was the supreme leader of the church. Before A.D. 1079, kings and nobles often influenced church appointments from the bishops up through the selection of the pope. After that year, only special members of the curia, cardinals, could elect the pope from among their own ranks.

MONASTICISM

Monasticism refers to a way of life in which one largely withdraws from the world in order to focus on spiritual growth. It became common in the Middle Ages among Christians who lived in special spiritual communities. Monks lived in monasteries, and nuns lived in convents. Most monasteries and convents followed the Benedictine Rule. These were guidelines developed by Benedict in the 500s. He had been a Roman Christian who was so repulsed by the sins of the Roman Empire that he retreated into the wilderness to live as a hermit. Many people admired his efforts and tried to emulate him. As Benedict's following grew, he established a monastery based on his rule of order.

Copyright © Mometrix Media. You have been licensed one copy of this document for personal use only. Any other reproduction or redistribution is strictly prohibited. All rights reserved.
This content is provided for test preparation purposes only and does not imply an endorsement by Mometrix of any particular political, scientific, or religious point of view.

This rule included a daily regimen that tried to balance prayer, manual labor, and study. It became the pattern for most monastic orders.

Life for Nuns

Nuns were among the most educated women in medieval society. Most came from the nobility. Unlike other noblewomen, nuns were taught to read and write and some became scholars themselves. Although they were not allowed to marry, nor have children, they were also not subjected to arranged marriages common of the times. Money that their families would have paid as dowries went instead to the church. Some widows chose to become nuns rather than remarry. Some nuns who became abbesses, leaders of convents, maintained powerful voices and influences on church practices.

Contributions of People to the Medieval Church

- Jerome — One of the earliest Biblical scholars; translated the Vulgate, the Latin version of the Bible adopted by the Catholic Church.
- Benedict — Established the Benedictine Rule that governed practices in all monasteries and convents
- Augustine — Leading Christian thinker of the early medieval era, his writings greatly shaped ideas about the role of the church in political affairs
- Patrick — Christian missionary who brought the faith to Ireland in the 400s.
- Gregory VII — Pope who tried to reform the church and end corruption caused by political influences;
- Innocent III — Most powerful of medieval popes; expanded papal power over European monarchies and political issues

The Three Orders

The three orders referred to those who work, those who fight, and those who pray.

1. Those who work. These were the peasants who made up the bulk of the population and kept the manors running. Their lives were usually short, difficult, and bound by the economic needs of the manor. Serfs had almost no rights under the law.
2. Those who fight. These were members of the nobility such as knights who led and protected kingdoms under feudalistic society. Their obligation was to serve the good of society. As long as they fulfilled their specific duties to their lord or king, they had a great deal of freedom. During this time most kings were also warriors.
3. Those who pray. These were the clergy who dedicated their lives to service of the church. The clergy were usually among the best-educated members of society, though they often lived simple lives with few material goods.

Influence of Chivalry

Chivalry was a code of conduct introduced to refine the behavior of knights, who served as defenders of feudal manors. It introduced many traditions that enhanced the romantic image of the knights. Chivalric knights were supposed to be brave and fierce in battle, but exhibit good manners and deference to others, especially noblewomen. As this idea expanded, the chivalric code developed into an elaborate system of rules to be followed primarily by knights to ensure that they fought fairly and with honor. Knights were supposed to be honest and loyal. They were also expected to treat their defeated enemies with compassion and respect. Each fought under a coat of arms that represented their kingdom, personality, and skills. A knight who violated the code was considered unworthy of respect. Knights and the chivalric code inspired most music and literature of the medieval period.

Copyright © Mometrix Media. You have been licensed one copy of this document for personal use only. Any other reproduction or redistribution is strictly prohibited. All rights reserved.
This content is provided for test preparation purposes only and does not imply an endorsement by Mometrix of any particular political, scientific, or religious point of view.

VERNACULAR LANGUAGE

Vernacular language referred to languages that people spoke in everyday life. Due to the lack of a centralized government or culture, medieval vernacular languages varied from community to community. Many evolved from Roman Latin, which was still the language of formal writing and of the Catholic Church. Since few Europeans could read or write, their spoken languages evolved to reflect their unique communities and ethnic identities. This diversification of vernacular languages and decrease in use of formal Latin would eventually play a role in church reform movements.

TROUBADOURS

Troubadours were travelling singers who wrote or memorized songs and poems and recited them as they travelled from town to town. In this way, troubadours helped preserve and spread medieval literature. Rather than reciting works in Latin, troubadours recited them in vernacular languages so that people could more easily understand them. Troubadours became popular entertainment among the nobility, often performing for women of the court. Their works reflected medieval chivalric romanticism, as well as veiled criticism of the culture.

GEOFFREY CHAUCER VS. DANTE

Both Chaucer and Dante wrote works in vernacular languages rather than Latin, reflecting their intent that they be understood by common people. Dante wrote his works in the language spoken around his home region of Tuscany, Italy, a form that eventually became the accepted written version of Italian. Dante's most famous work, *The Divine Comedy,* was completed around 1321, in which he described a Christian journey through three stages of the afterlife – hell, purgatory, and heaven. *The Divine Comedy* reflected the influence of Catholicism on the writer, but also served as a means to satirize political leadership in Italy. England's Geoffrey Chaucer wrote in the vernacular language of Middle English. His most famous work, *The Canterbury Tales,* written in the 1390s, describes a spiritual pilgrimage of a group of Christians. Like Dante, Chaucer used his work to criticize leadership, but was much harder on corrupt church officials, showing how some were more concerned with making money than in leading a spiritual life.

THOMAS AQUINAS

Thomas Aquinas was a priest who emerged as one of the most important philosophers of the 1200s. He was part of a philosophical movement called scholasticism that tried to bridge the gap between faith and reason. An admirer of Aristotle, Aquinas sought to increase appreciation for ancient Greek thought within the church. His most famous work was the *Summa Theologica,* in which he offered a rationalized defense for the existence of God, support for modified Aristotelian ethics, and an explanation of Christ's meaning in the world. Many scholars consider this work the best summation of medieval theology. After Aquinas's death, supporters of his theological writings adopted his approach as Thomism.

INFLUENCE OF ROMANESQUE AND GOTHIC STYLES ON MEDIEVAL ARCHITECTURE

Both styles are reflected mainly in medieval church architecture. Romanesque attempted to recreate styles common in the Roman Empire, with heavy, domed stone roofs, low walls, few windows, and poor lighting. This style was very common in structures built between the years 1000 and 1150. Around 1150, a new style emerged that was much more ornamental, designed to reflect the awesome glory of God, with most elements pointing skyward towards heaven. Supporting structures called flying buttresses redistributed the weight of the roof through the use of arches, allowing for high, thin walls. Within these high walls were large stained glass windows that portrayed holy figures or stories from the Bible. The windows also allowed more light, brightening the interiors. Many gothic churches were also decorated with statues of holy figures. Critics of this

Copyright © Mometrix Media. You have been licensed one copy of this document for personal use only. Any other reproduction or redistribution is strictly prohibited. All rights reserved.
This content is provided for test preparation purposes only and does not imply an endorsement by Mometrix of any particular political, scientific, or religious point of view.

new style derisively called it "gothic" after the barbarian Goths who destroyed ancient Roman architecture when they invaded Europe in the 400s. Although the architectural styles did not originate with the Goths, the nickname stuck.

Medieval Universities

Since most of the population was illiterate, formal education was reserved only for certain members of the nobility and the clergy. While many were tutored by private instructors, schools for the nobility developed in some areas. As professional guilds arose, educational guilds were formed, called universitas, or "association of people" to represent the interests of schools. From these guilds emerged a movement to create schools of higher learning for those who desired further study in certain specialties. The first four major European universities were Paris and Oxford, which both taught theology and liberal arts; the University of Bologna, which focused on civil and church law; and the University at Salerno, which focused on medical training.

Affect of Trade on Medieval Economy

Due to a combination of factors, global trade virtually collapsed after the fall of the Roman Empire. The Crusades reopened trade routes and sparked renewed interest in foreign goods. Cities with access to ports and land routes to Asia emerged as centers of trade. Lacking centralized governments to regulate trade, groups such as the Germanic Hanseatic League emerged to fulfill this role. The leagues used their economic power as a political tool, sometimes cutting off supply lines to cities whose leaders would not comply with their policies. Interest in new goods gave rise to market-based economies within trade cities. Traders exchanged desired goods and services through a barter system. In exchange for providing protection, some local rulers taxed a portion of the traded goods. Soon some local rulers began to issue currency to represent the value of goods. The need for manufactured goods and services also gave rise to new industries and jobs within towns.

Emergence of the Banking Industry

As local leaders began to issue their own currency, moneychangers arose to establish values and rates of exchange at fairs and other centers of trade. They collected a portion back through fees. In time, the role of the moneychangers expanded to include loaning money to others, including nobles and kings. Moneychangers not bound by the church edicts against usury charged interest on these loans. To represent the loans, moneychangers issued bills of exchange, which served as a type of pre-modern check accepted by moneychangers in other regions. Loaned money was often used to invest in new economic ventures, which further expanded the market economy. Eventually the money-changing system evolved into banking. The word "bank" comes from the Italian term *banca,* literally meaning "moneychanger's bench."

Rise of Medieval Towns

With the expansion of trade, people who were not involved with manorial farming began to gather in centralized areas to run the market economy. Merchants, moneychangers, and those in other jobs directly related to trade soon fueled the need for laborers to fulfill other jobs. Agricultural innovations such as the deep plow allowed for greater production to feed larger populations. Rather than merely being self-sufficient, farmers now had excess produce to sell to non-agrarian workers. With less need for laborers, nobles allowed some serfs to leave the manors to seek work in towns. Many became artisans, producing goods or services for others townsfolk.

Medieval Town Charters

Even as market economies expanded, nobles from nearby manors still influenced town governments. In some towns, residents rebelled against nobles whom they felt were not treating

Copyright © Mometrix Media. You have been licensed one copy of this document for personal use only. Any other reproduction or redistribution is strictly prohibited. All rights reserved.
This content is provided for test preparation purposes only and does not imply an endorsement by Mometrix of any particular political, scientific, or religious point of view.

them fairly or who were trying to limit their profits. In some regions, these conflicts erupted into violent protests. To limit such conflicts, some nobles began to allow the creation of town charters, which granted certain rights and liberties to residents. Such charters typically came to include several basic rights of citizens designed to limit the power of the nobles. Indentured serfs who resided within towns for at least one year automatically became free citizens, able to work for whomever they pleased and to travel wherever they pleased. Town citizens could not be forced to work on manor property, nor pay taxes to nobles. Legal issues involving town citizens were decided by local courts, not manor nobles. Town citizens had the right to trade their goods freely in the marketplace and charge non-citizens for the right to trade in their town.

Emergence of Guilds

Guilds, associations of people from similar professions, helped strengthen their members' positions within the new economy. Guilds arose because the rise of towns and the expansion of trade which created a need for new professions. Two of the most common types of guilds were the merchant guilds and craft guilds. Merchant guilds controlled trade within specific towns. Anyone wanting to trade within that area had to join or pay a fee to the guild, which made sure the traders maintained certain standards. Guilds sometimes served as banks, offering loans to guild members. Craft guilds were made up of members of the same artisan profession. Guilds set standards for training, wages, working conditions, and product quality. Under guilds, a system of apprenticeship developed to train new workers in the craft. Because most jobs within the new economy were reserved for men, both merchant and craft guilds provided financial support to widows and orphans when a guild member died. They also lobbied local government on behalf of their profession.

Affect of Economic Change on Social Classes

Within the manor system, there were typically two classes: the nobility and the peasantry. These social classes were very rigid and passed down through heredity. The rise of the town-based market economy brought with it the rise of a new middle class made up of traders, moneychangers, artisans, and service providers. The middle class was more fluid than the manorial classes. One could move up or down based on the amount of wealth one could generate. This wealth could change from generation to generation. In time, members of the middle class began to challenge and weaken the political influence of the nobility by demanding governmental policies which favored the new economic and social structures over the old traditions of feudalism and manorialism.

Black Death

The rapid rise in trade and growth of towns led to a new exchange of germs within often unsanitary, crowded urban areas and then spread to rural communities. The plague that became known as the Black Death is believed to have been brought to Europe from Asia aboard trading vessels which contained plague-infested rats. The worst outbreak lasted from 1347 to 1351, killing some 25 million people throughout Europe. As a result, the populations of some entire towns disappeared. Faith in the church decreased. The large loss of life among peasant laborers forced some landowners to offer wages and incentives to attract workers, further boosting the market economy over the traditional manorial system. Social classes became more fluid as surviving peasants filled the skilled laborer positions vacated when workers died.

Review Video: Black Death (An Overview)
Visit mometrix.com/academy and enter code: 431857

Viking Influence

The Vikings emerged from Scandinavia as one of the most feared and powerful of the invading Germanic forces during the 800s and 900s. The Vikings established settlements throughout Europe,

Copyright © Mometrix Media. You have been licensed one copy of this document for personal use only. Any other reproduction or redistribution is strictly prohibited. All rights reserved.
This content is provided for test preparation purposes only and does not imply an endorsement by Mometrix of any particular political, scientific, or religious point of view.

including the French region of Normandy. They established a strong foothold in England in the late 800s. The Viking threat united the Wessex kingdom under Alfred the Great, who built a powerful army and navy to repel the Vikings (whom they called "Danes"). In 886, after ten years of fighting, the Danes surrendered. Alfred allowed them their own independent kingdoms in Mercia and Northumbria. In time, the Danes attempted to retake control of England and succeeded in taking the empire of Canute, until a new Anglo-Saxon king emerged in 1042. Fierce warriors and superior seafarers, the Vikings explored far more regions than other Europeans of this time, including parts of North America.

Anglo-Saxon Culture and Rule

After Roman forces withdrew from the British Isles in A.D. 450, competing Germanic tribes struggled for control of the region. The Angles and Saxons emerged as the dominant forces, giving rise to what became known as the Anglo-Saxon culture. The numerous small Anglo-Saxon kingdoms shared many common features, including the dialect now called Old English. The southern province of Wessex emerged as the strongest of the Anglo-Saxon kingdoms. Wessex king Alfred the Great succeeded in defeating Vikings forces in 886. By Alfred's reign, most Anglo-Saxon regions had organized into shires, or counties, led by officials known as ealdormen and shire-reeves. These positions evolved into aldermen and sheriffs of later cultures.

Turning Point in European History

With the decline of Danish power in England, the Anglo-Saxons solidified their power by naming Edward the Confessor as king in 1042. When Edward died in 1066 without an heir, a struggle for power emerged. Edward's distant relative, William of Normandy, was one of many who claimed a right to the throne. By this time French Normandy was a powerful kingdom in continental Europe. Anglo-Saxon nobles, who did not want to see England absorbed into Norman culture, placed Harold of Wessex on the throne. William led his forces across the English Channel to meet Harold's forces in the Battle of Hastings on October 14, 1066. William the Conqueror won the battle and was soon crowned king of England. He brought Norman customs and strong monarchical feudalism to the island, forever changing the course of European history.

Thomas Becket and Eleanor of Aquitaine

Henry II, grandson of William the Conqueror, ruled England from 1154 to 1189. During that time, he took many steps, such as collecting fees from nobles to support an army loyal to the king, to strengthen the power of the monarchy. He also challenged church authority by insisting that clergy accused of crimes be tried in royal courts. Thomas Becket, the archbishop of Canterbury who had previously supported Henry, opposed this policy, arguing that only church courts had the authority to try clergy. When members of Henry's court murdered Becket, the backlash against the monarch was so strong that Henry was forced to revise his stance against church power. In 1152, Henry married Eleanor of Aquitaine, the former queen consort of France. Eleanor played an influential role in his court, even supporting the failed rebellion of his sons against Henry.

Magna Carta

King John, son of Henry II, tried to increase taxes against nobles to support the English war against France. In 1215, an influential group of nobles led a rebellion against the king that threatened to topple the monarchy. In exchange for remaining in power, John signed the Magna Carta, meaning "Great Charter," which provided specific rights to citizens, including the right of habeas corpus. More importantly, the Magna Carta established the precedent that even monarchs should be bound by the rule of law. The document inspired many subsequent constitutions and statements on the liberties of the people and limits on monarchy.

Copyright © Mometrix Media. You have been licensed one copy of this document for personal use only. Any other reproduction or redistribution is strictly prohibited. All rights reserved.
This content is provided for test preparation purposes only and does not imply an endorsement by Mometrix of any particular political, scientific, or religious point of view.

PARLIAMENTARY LAW AND COMMON LAW

The signing of the Magna Carta increased the role of the nobility in government. In the 1260s, Simon de Montfort led an uprising among both the nobility and the emerging middle class to seek an even greater voice. Beginning in 1265, representatives of the middle class joined the Great Council. Each shire or township was allowed to seat a certain number of representatives. Eventually this representative body became the English Parliament, split into an upper house, comprised of nobles and clergy, and a lower house comprised of knights and burgesses (leading town citizens). Parliament's greatest power was its ability to approve taxes. Edward I, who ruled from 1272 to 1307, strengthened the rule of common law, or law based on customs and judicial rulings instead of written codes alone. Edward established three major court systems to deal with legal issues. Those court decisions became the basis for rulings throughout the land, though unlike written laws, common law was fluid and more easily adaptable to change over time.

EVENTS UNDER THE CAPETIAN KINGS

- When the last Carolingian king died in 987, French nobles chose Henry Capet as leader of the kingdom centered near Ile-de-France. Henry's descendents sought to expand their monarchy and unify all of the French kingdoms under one central government.
- Capetian leader Philip II (1180-1223) drove most of the English nobles out of western France.
- Philip IV (1285-1314) challenged church authority by taxing the clergy, leading to the Great Schism. Philip also convened the Estates General in 1302, a governing body representing the three main French social classes—commoners, nobles, and clergy. By giving people a voice in government, he secured public support in his fight against the church.
- In 1328, the last of the Capetians, Charles IV, died without an heir, ending the family's line. Despite the expansion of power under the Capetians, they never achieved their goal of fully unifying the French people, most of whom still recognized local kingdoms.

HUNDRED YEARS' WAR

In 1328, Charles IV, the last Capetian king of France, died without an heir. English king Edward III claimed the throne, but French officials selected Philip IV of Flanders instead. In 1337, Edward III led an English army against Flanders, sparking a war that would continue off and on until 1453. Eventually France won the war, securing control of all English-held French lands except for the small region of Calais. The conflict led to a huge loss of male population as it produced many deadly innovations in warfare, such as use of the longbow, gunpowder, and cannons. In England, the war strengthened the power of Parliament when members of the House of Commons, protesting handling of the war, sought and received a greater voice in advising the king and collecting taxes for warfare. The war had the opposite effect in France, where the power of the Estates General weakened, leading to the strong, dictatorial-style of monarchy established by Louis XI in 1461.

WAR OF THE ROSES

The War of the Roses was a battle for control of the English throne that lasted from 1455 to 1485. It was fought between the York and Lancaster families. The conflict became known as the War of the Roses because the York family seal was a white rose and the Lancaster family seal was a red rose. Prior to the war, the country suffered through a series of weak rulers which threatened the country's security. Various factions rose up to support control by either the Yorks or the Lancasters, both of whom claimed rightful control through their common ancestor Edward III. Power shifted back and forth as the two houses struggled for power. The war finally ended when Henry Tudor (a Lancaster) defeated Richard III (a York) to take control of the throne. To strengthen his rule, he

Copyright © Mometrix Media. You have been licensed one copy of this document for personal use only. Any other reproduction or redistribution is strictly prohibited. All rights reserved.
This content is provided for test preparation purposes only and does not imply an endorsement by Mometrix of any particular political, scientific, or religious point of view.

married Elizabeth of York, creating a united throne of both houses. Under the control of the Tudors, England developed a strong and powerful monarchy.

Joan of Arc

Joan was born a French peasant around 1412, in the midst of the Hundred Years' War. In 1428, she reported experiencing visions from saints telling her to lead French forces against the English. During the course of several attempts to meet with the dauphin Charles, who was trying to secure the crown, many French people came to believe in her piety. Church officials who examined Joan advised Charles to trust her. She led a miraculous victory against the English at the Battle of Orleans in May 1429. This and other victories helped secure the coronation of Charles VII. In 1431, she was captured by political enemies and brought before an inquisition on charges of heresy. Found guilty, she was executed on May 30. Yet she remained a heroine to the French people, who dedicated the anniversary of her death as a day of remembrance for her courage and loyalty. She was canonized in 1920 and remains an honored French and Catholic heroine.

Habsburg dynasty

In 1273, Rudolf I of the Habsburg family became Holy Roman Emperor at a time when the title had lost much of its power. Initially his court only controlled a small area of land in what is now Switzerland. Over the years, the Habsburg heirs leveraged the title of Holy Roman Emperor to arrange marriages and achieve minor military victories that slowly expanded their land holdings in central Europe. Under Habsburg leader Maximilian I, the family acquired control of the Netherlands, Luxembourg, and Burgundy. Their tradition of politically influenced marriages ensconced Habsburg kin in most of the European monarchies. By the 1400s, the Habsburgs were the most powerful ruling family in Europe.

Crusades

As the Muslim Seljuk Turks expanded their empire, they seized control of Palestine, or the Holy Land, an area sacred to Christians, Muslims, and Jews. When the Seljuks expanded into the Byzantine Empire and threatened Constantinople, Byzantine leaders sought help from western forces through an appeal to Pope Urban II. In 1095, Urban called upon western Christian forces to not only aid the Byzantines, but also to launch a holy crusade against the Muslims to retake control of Palestine. The cause led to a series of wars over control of the Holy Land. In the long run, the crusades failed to maintain Christian control of Palestine, but they forever changed Europe. They introduced new weapons, such as the crossbow and catapult, and shifted power, as many nobles were killed during the fighting. The power of the church increased due to the unifying nature of the cause. Returning crusaders brought back new ideas and interest in eastern trade goods, which helped give rise to the new market economy.

Crusades

- First Crusade – 1096-1099. Inspired by Urban II's call for a holy war, crusaders protected Constantinople, and then overtook Muslim forces to reclaim control of Jerusalem. After the victory the crusaders massacred many Muslims and Jews within the city, established feudalistic systems, and opened trade routes with the east.
- Second Crusade – 1147-1149. When Turkish forces began retaking cities throughout Palestine, French King Louis VII and German King Conrad III led two crusading armies into the region. The European forces met up against the Turks at Damascus, but suffered an embarrassing defeat.

Copyright © Mometrix Media. You have been licensed one copy of this document for personal use only. Any other reproduction or redistribution is strictly prohibited. All rights reserved.
This content is provided for test preparation purposes only and does not imply an endorsement by Mometrix of any particular political, scientific, or religious point of view.

- Third Crusade – 1189-1192. After Muslim leader Saladin took control of Jerusalem, three European forces led by Holy Roman Emperor Frederick Barbarossa, French King Philip II, and English King Richard I launched a crusade. Barbarossa's army turned back after his death. Philip and Richard disagreed, leading Philip to withdraw his army and attack England. Richard reclaimed some lands and negotiated a truce with Saladin that allowed for free passage for Christians into Jerusalem.

Children's Crusade

The Children's Crusade was an aberrant movement in which thousands of young people across Europe declared their intention to launch a new crusade to retake Jerusalem. The exact origins of the movement are unknown and possibly mythological, but it allegedly lasted from May until September of 1212. None of the young people appears to have reached Palestine and many never returned home. Legend claimed that some were wrongly sold into slavery. The religious fervor sparked by the movement continued and possibly inspired the Fifth Crusade in 1218. Some historians credit the Children's Crusade as an early example of a youth movement, though others doubt its veracity.

Inquisition

Concerns that rising Christian sects were undermining church authority led the pope to grant bishops the power of inquisition, or church trial for heresy, in 1184. The power was not widely used until Pope Gregory IX appointed a special delegation of friars to conduct inquisitions in 1227. These inquisitors had investigative power over almost all almost Catholic subjects except bishops. The loosely organized judges codified their practices in a manual written around 1249. In 1252, Pope Innocent IV sanctioned the use of torture against suspected heretics. This inquisition succeeded in suppressing reform movements critical of the church as well as popular new sects such as the Cathars and Waldenses. It also established an acceptance for the use of torture that influenced later anti-heretical movements.

Great Schism

The Great Schism was a theological and political debate which weakened the political influence of the Catholic Church in Europe. As monarchies of rising nation-states grew in power, some kings began to reject the church's political influence. This tension was particularly strong in France, where King Philip IV struggled with Pope Boniface VIII regarding which one held the highest authority. After Boniface died in 1303, Philip used his political clout to make sure a French bishop whom he could control was elected pope. The church's headquarters moved from Rome to Avignon, France. For many years French popes reigned from Avignon. When the French pope died in Italy in 1378, the cardinals first elected an Italian pope, then later a second French pope. At one time, the church had three popes, each elected to appease political factions and controlling different regions. A church council in 1414 resolved the conflict and elected a new pope, but the church never regained the political influence it had maintained before the Great Schism.

Babylonian Captivity

The Babylonian Captivity describes the period in church history between 1309 and 1377, when the Catholic popes were headquartered in Avignon, France, rather than in Rome. Opponents of the move, who rightly believed the Avignon popes were being controlled by the French monarchy, opposed what they felt was the subjugation of the church to secular rulers. The era was so named after a roughly 70-year period described in the Bible when the ancient Hebrews were forced to live in exile under heathen rule in Babylon. The era of Babylonian Captivity preceded the Great Schism.

Copyright © Mometrix Media. You have been licensed one copy of this document for personal use only. Any other reproduction or redistribution is strictly prohibited. All rights reserved.
This content is provided for test preparation purposes only and does not imply an endorsement by Mometrix of any particular political, scientific, or religious point of view.

Francis of Assisi

Born around 1182, Francis was a monk who in 1207 felt called to a life of complete poverty and service to the lowliest classes of society. Others heeded his call, leading to the establishment of the Franciscan order that included friars as well as the nuns of St. Clare. Franciscans attempted to emulate the life of Jesus Christ, traveling to spread the gospel, aiding the poor and sick, and refusing financial rewards of any kind. The movement proved extremely popular, attracting thousands by the time of Francis's death in 1226.

John Wycliffe and Jan Hus

Wycliffe and Hus were reformers who opposed what they felt was a corruption of faith within the Catholic Church. Wycliffe, an English priest and teacher at Oxford University, believed that too much power was vested in the pope and the clergy. A proponent for the expansion of literacy, Wycliffe felt that people should be able to read and interpret the Bible for themselves. He helped bring about the first English translation of the Bible. Tried as a heretic, but saved from death by powerful supporters, Wycliffe was forced to retire in 1381. The reformist group the Lollards continued to propagate his views. Jan Hus was a Czech teacher at the University of Prague and advocate of Wycliffe's teachings. Hus was first tried as a heretic and exiled, then tried again and burned at the stake in 1415. Both reformers foreshadowed later, stronger movements for reform within the church.

Terms

- canon law — code of law that guided the Catholic Church; enforced by church courts with the power of excommunication
- interdict — Power of the church courts to cut off an entire region from receiving the sacraments and other benefits of church membership; usually used against a community whose secular leader was opposing church authority; purpose was to get common people united in opposition to the wayward ruler
- heretic — person who did not believe in or follow church policy; considered a threat to church power and worthy of eternal damnation
- tithe — tenth of one's income; collected by parish priests to help support the work of the church
- lay investiture — Practice of secular leaders appointing Catholic bishops; often based on kinship or political needs
- simony — Practice of one person paying a noble to appoint them to a position of power within the church

Copyright © Mometrix Media. You have been licensed one copy of this document for personal use only. Any other reproduction or redistribution is strictly prohibited. All rights reserved.
This content is provided for test preparation purposes only and does not imply an endorsement by Mometrix of any particular political, scientific, or religious point of view.

Renaissance and Reformation

Renaissance

The word "renaissance" means "rebirth." The nearly 1000-year period between the fall of the Roman Empire and the Renaissance are sometimes referred to as the Dark Ages because communication, travel, and education generally decreased as tribalism and localism took over much of the western world. Many of the great literary, philosophical, and artistic contributions of the Romans and Greeks were ignored, if not forgotten. The Renaissance marked renewed interest in these ancient cultures, leading to a flourishing of intellectual and artistic endeavors.

The Renaissance began in Italy, as the Crusades helped reopen trade routes and brought Italians into greater contact with the Byzantine Empire. The Byzantines, who revered Roman and Greek thought, had preserved many of the ancient writings and art that had been lost in Europe during foreign invasions. As descendents of the ancient Romans, Italian leaders particularly encouraged a rebirth of intellectual thought and artistry.

Humanist Philosophy and Influence

The humanists were a school of secular thinkers who first emerged in Italy in the 1300s to study classical works of ancient Greece and Rome. They focused on four major areas: Greek and Latin grammar, history, poetry, and rhetoric (the humanities). The humanists meticulously studied ancient manuscripts, some of which were preserved originals and many of which were copies. They developed a system for comparing manuscripts in order to determine which were the most authentic. Their desire to determine authenticity in manuscripts led to further study. The humanists laid the foundation for much of the learning of the Renaissance. Their name derives from the philosophical theories they developed about humanity. They stressed the study of human nature and dignity of humans; developed syncretism, which strove to find commonalities among philosophical and theological systems; and promoted a rebirth of what they felt was a lost human spirit and wisdom which could only be gained through learning.

Classical Education

Classical education evolved out of the humanist movement. It focused on detailed study and emulation of ancient Greek and Roman writers. A classical education focused on reading and writing the ancient Greek and Latin languages. More than merely translating and transcribing texts, students tried to understand how ancient writers thought. The students then tried to develop their own original works based on the knowledge passed on by ancient masters. Thus students built upon ancient teachings. The study of ancient Greek and Latin writings is still referred to as "Classics" today.

Renaissance Art

Italian merchants and bankers established the precedent for the patronage system. The post-Crusades opening of trade created a new class of wealthy market-based business leaders in trade cities such as Florence. Nationalist interest in restoring the pride of Italian art and thinking led many of these wealthy individuals to invest their money in the arts. Patron families backed specific artists or schools and usually adorned their homes with images created by their supported visual artists. Many families accumulated impressive private art collections, some of which they later donated to the state for public viewing. As support for the arts expanded, monarchs and religious leaders became patrons themselves, further expanding the Renaissance. The most important patron family was the Medici of Florence, originating from Cosimo Medici's support for artistic and

Copyright © Mometrix Media. You have been licensed one copy of this document for personal use only. Any other reproduction or redistribution is strictly prohibited. All rights reserved.
This content is provided for test preparation purposes only and does not imply an endorsement by Mometrix of any particular political, scientific, or religious point of view.

educational projects in the 1400s. Medici's personal regard for artists helped increase respect for the profession and encouraged patronage among other wealthy families.

Works of Petrarch, Machiavelli, and Castiglione

- Francesco Petrarch — Humanist scholar and poet who focused on the need to live a virtuous life and avoid temptations of fame; promoted development of Renaissance lyric poetry; wrote love sonnets to Laura, an ideal woman
- Niccolo Machiavelli — Diplomat and historian who rejected idealism of writers like Petrarch; preferred to emulate the ruthless behavior of ancient Roman leaders; wrote *The Prince* (1513), a pragmatic approach to governing which advised rulers to be concerned mainly with maintaining their own power; spawned term "Machiavellian" to describe a ruthless politician; credited with birthing philosophy of modernity
- Baldassare Castiglione — Diplomat and writer who used voices of observers to reveal insights into royal and governmental events; wrote *The Courtier* (1528), a portrayal of real individuals engaged in a fictional story to describe how nobles should behave; mixture of historical actors with fiction made the book very popular among the educated classes.

Medieval vs. Renaissance Art

Medieval arts (which did exist despite the image of the Dark Ages) tended to be very otherworldly and formal, incorporating imaginative images of even real events and places. Early paintings depicting the Crusades, for example, tended to be rather flat and cartoonish, reflecting nothing realistic about the historical sites where battles took place. Because most art during this time was church-sponsored, it dealt almost exclusively with religious themes. Renaissance artists focused intensely on realism in visual arts, using perspective, shading, and light to better reflect the real physical world. Even holy figures, such as the Virgin Mary and Jesus, were portrayed as realistically as possible, emphasizing their humanity as well as their sanctity. Moreover, while religious themes remained important to Renaissance artists, they also incorporated secular themes and subjects to a much greater extent than medieval artists had. Some artists also emulated themes of classical works, including ancient mythology, gods, and goddesses.

Brunelleschi, Masaccio, Ghiberti, and Botticelli

All were pioneering artists from Florence whose works set the standards for much of the Renaissance art that followed.

- Filippo Brunelleschi — Architect and engineer in the early 1400s who pioneered Renaissance styles of building construction; invented construction machines invaluable to massive new projects; greatest work was the Cathedral of Santa Maria del Fiore (the Duomo) in Florence
- Masaccio — Painter whose frescoes in the Brancacci Chapel shaped move towards realism; utilized scientific understandings of anatomy, tried to improve perspective, use of space, and lighting; career cut short by early death, but works studied extensively by later artists
- Lorenzo Ghiberti — Sculptor and art historian who became master at creating images in various metals; famed for religious figures and incorporation of sculpture in architecture; noted works include "Gates of Paradise," doors for the Baptistery of the cathedral of Florence; *Commentarii* detailed history of art from antiquity to Ghiberti's own life
- Sandro Botticelli — Painter; study of classics and humanism influenced works, which celebrated voluptuous physical beauty; art school shaped spirit of the Renaissance; noted works include *Primavera* and *Birth of Venus.*

Copyright © Mometrix Media. You have been licensed one copy of this document for personal use only. Any other reproduction or redistribution is strictly prohibited. All rights reserved.
This content is provided for test preparation purposes only and does not imply an endorsement by Mometrix of any particular political, scientific, or religious point of view.

Leonardo Da Vinci

As the Renaissance expanded, education and knowledge flourished in a variety of fields. Da Vinci was one of the few who excelled in a multitude of these fields. He was an accomplished engineer, architect, painter, sculptor, and scientist who constantly experimented by trying to gather new information and improve his work in every field. Leonardo developed the philosophy that art and science should work together. He studied anatomy to improve his artistic representations of the human body. He also incorporated his knowledge of mathematics to improve balance and perspective within paintings. He made detailed sketches of his designs for numerous inventions, some of which he built and others which remained only theoretical. Some of his theoretical inventions that later became real included a flying machine and a submarine. Leonardo's most famous paintings include *The Last Supper* and *Mona Lisa.*

Michelangelo

Michelangelo was one of the most famous artists during the Renaissance, and is still considered one of the greatest artists of all time. Michelangelo was a painter, sculptor, and architect. Unlike many contemporaries who employed assistants to complete works, Michelangelo usually insisted on carrying out his own work, which left some projects incomplete or took them years to finish. The artist is famous for clashing with Pope Julius II regarding the Sistine Chapel. Michelangelo's most famous works include:

- *Pieta* (1499): marble sculpture depicting the Virgin Mary holding the body of Jesus after his crucifixion
- *David* (1504): nude marble sculpture of Biblical figure David prior to his encounter with Goliath; represented strength of Florence; placed in seat of government
- Frescoes on the ceiling of the Sistine Chapel (1508-1512), particularly scenes from the Book of Genesis; massive, detailed work unprecedented in scope and grandeur
- *The Last Judgment* (1537-1541): fresco on altar wall of the Sistine Chapel; portrays prophesied second coming of Christ and Apocalypse; highly controversial for dark, graphic imagery placed within a sacred space

Artistic Styles of Giotto, Raphael, Titian, Tintoretto, and Palladio

- Giotto — Extremely realistic painter; legend says that a fly in one painting looked so real an observer tried to brush it off the painting; works include decoration of Arena Chapel (1305)
- Raphael — Accomplished painter of religious imagery; known mainly for his church frescoes, madonnas, and cherubs
- Titian — Painter with very dramatic, colorful style; works include *Assumption of the Virgin* (1506)
- Tintoretto — Considered last of the great Renaissance painters; works reflected haunting realism; most famous works include group of religious painting made for Scuola di San Rocca (1565-1588)
- Palladio — Venetian architect, 1500s; promoted incorporation of ancient Roman styles in Renaissance buildings; largely responsible for the classical styles popular in public buildings

Copyright © Mometrix Media. You have been licensed one copy of this document for personal use only. Any other reproduction or redistribution is strictly prohibited. All rights reserved.
This content is provided for test preparation purposes only and does not imply an endorsement by Mometrix of any particular political, scientific, or religious point of view.

Philosophies of Erasmus and Thomas More

Both Erasmus and More were close friends and humanists who flourished in the early 1500s and influenced much humanist thought that followed.

- Erasmus — Dutch humanist; combined classics with early Christian studies; wrote *The Praise of Folly* (1511), critical of many contemporary Christian practices, including fasting, pilgrimages, Biblical interpretations, and general reliance upon superstition over reason.
- More — English humanist; agreed with Erasmus; focused more on government behavior; wrote *Utopia* (1516), depicting ideal society in which all men were equal and there was no ownership of private property; worked for King Henry VIII, but remained devout Catholic; beheaded for refusing to recognize the king as head of the Anglican Church.

William Shakespeare

Shakespeare was an English playwright and poet who flourished during the late 1500s and early 1600s. He came to prominence during a time when the theater was gaining in popularity. Shakespeare wrote numerous plays in a variety of genres, including histories, tragedies, and comedies. He was one of the first successful writers to combine romance and tragedy. Shakespeare's masterful use of language and vivid characterizations made him not only the foremost writer of his day, but he is generally considered one of the greatest writers of all time. His works have been translated into nearly every major language and performed throughout the globe, a testament to his universal themes. While financially successful in his time, Shakespeare exhibited a greater influence on later writers, particularly 19th century Romantics, who emulated his language and themes.

Flemish School

The Flemish School consisted of a group of painters from Flanders who developed a unique visual style grounded in realism. They painted mostly in oils on canvas. Leading members of the Flemish School included:

- Jan and Hubert van Eyck — brothers who created very detailed images, with particular attention paid to human faces; perfected method of painting with oils; major works include Jan's *The Arnolfini Portrait* (1434), a widely studied image of a couple
- Pieter Brueghel — known as Peter the Elder; focused on rural settings, images of peasants; works often served to criticize social injustices he observed; works include *Children's Games* (1560) and *Winter Landscape with Bird Trap* (1565)
- Gerard David — painted and illustrated many manuscripts, leading to work in miniatures; renowned for brilliant use of colors; works include *Virgin among Virgins* (1509)

Albrecht Dürer and Hans Holbein the Younger

Both were German artists who promoted and elevated the arts in their region. Drürer was a painter and printer who combined study of the classics and humanism with art. He created numerous copper engravings and woodcuts, which he used to show the possibilities of illustrations in printed books. His works include the Goth-inspired *Apocalypse* series (1498).

Holbein, son of a renowned Gothic artist, was more heavily influenced by Italian artists, the Flemish School, and the humanist movement. He illustrated *The Praise of Folly* for Erasmus as well as Martin Luther's German Bible. Holbein became famous as a portrait painter, reflecting the Renaissance focus on the greatness of individual men. Holbein became so famous he was contracted to paint the portraits of English dignitaries, including members of the court of English King Henry VIII.

Copyright © Mometrix Media. You have been licensed one copy of this document for personal use only. Any other reproduction or redistribution is strictly prohibited. All rights reserved.
This content is provided for test preparation purposes only and does not imply an endorsement by Mometrix of any particular political, scientific, or religious point of view.

Popular Theater during the Renaissance

Public performances were popular throughout the medieval era, though most were carried out by performers who traveled to small audiences. During the early Renaissance, interest in the arts and Classics lent support to the creation of fixed theaters, such as those that had been popular in ancient Greece and Rome. The new buildings encouraged the gathering of audiences for large-scale performances. Public theater became particularly popular in England, offering diversions for the growing urban populations which were centered around London. Several popular theaters, including William Shakespeare's Globe Theatre, sprang up near the city. Most theaters followed a similar design of three stories of seating around a central stage area. They employed companies of actors who performed numerous plays so that there was a constant influx of new materials to draw in audiences. Companies were all-male, with younger members playing female roles. Audience participation and commentary were encouraged, turning some performances into rowdy, raucous experiences. While some nobles looked upon theaters with disdain, the institution proved to be one of the forerunners of popular mass entertainment.

Unification of Spain

Spain represented the bulk of lands on the Iberian Peninsula, which for centuries was divided into five kingdoms, with the large, centrally located Castile taking up the majority of land. Northeastern Aragon was the second-largest kingdom, followed by western Portugal, southern Granada, and tiny northern Navarre. The unification began when Ferdinand of Aragon married Isabella of Castile in 1469, uniting their kingdoms. Ferdinand and Isabella began a process of modernization to strengthen Spain's economy and military. They also instituted the Inquisition, to ensure Spain remained a Catholic nation. In 1492, Ferdinand and Isabella gained control of Granada when Spanish troops drove out the dominant Moors. That same year, they launched the Reconquista, an effort to drive out all non-Catholics. The policy primarily affected Jews and Muslims, who made up significant populations in some regions. In 1515, Ferdinand and Isabella completed the unification by annexing Navarre. Portugal, which had unsuccessfully tried to lay claim to Castile, remained independent.

Leadership of Kievan Russia

Kievan Russia refers to the Orthodox Christian kingdom centered near the city of Kiev (now in the Ukraine), then dominated by the descendant of the Rus. Because of its proximity to the Byzantine Empire, Kievan Russia developed significant trade routes which flourished even during the Middle Ages when there was little major trade in Europe. Wealth from trade allowed Kiev to build beautiful public buildings showcasing early Russian artistry. The Cathedral of St. Sophia stands as the only lasting example of this architecture, revealing influences from various cultures. Most buildings in Kiev were destroyed in later wars. Beginning in the late Middle Ages, Kievan Russia began to decline due to infighting among its leaders. Without a strong, centralized government, the princes who led small towns and villages engaged in wars to expand their holdings. Groups like the Turkish Polovsty and merchants from rising Italian city-states seized Russian trade routes. Soon Kiev itself began to weaken, subject to numerous attacks, even by other Russians who hoped that by weakening the capital they could increase their own power.

Affect of Mongol control on Russia

The Mongols were a warrior nation which originated in the Asian area east of the Ural Mountains. In 1206, Mongol leader Genghis Khan unified all of the Mongol tribes, and then launched invasions into other lands to expand territory for Mongol settlement. Correctly sensing that Russia's civil unrest left it vulnerable to attack, the Mongols invaded and took control of most of Kievan Russia, destroying the capital in 1240. The Mongols controlled Russia for more than 200 years. During that

Copyright © Mometrix Media. You have been licensed one copy of this document for personal use only. Any other reproduction or redistribution is strictly prohibited. All rights reserved.
This content is provided for test preparation purposes only and does not imply an endorsement by Mometrix of any particular political, scientific, or religious point of view.

time, they levied high taxes on the Russians. Since their main desire was for wealth, the Mongols allowed local areas to maintain their own governments and churches as long as they prospered economically and met their tax obligations. Still, the presence of Mongols changed Russian culture, mixing Mongol words, clothing, and customs with traditional Slavic culture. The Orthodox Church, however, retained its central position among the population.

Reign of the Ivans

As foreign wars weakened the Mongol Empire, Russian princes regained power. Muscovy, later "Moscow," emerged as the most powerful principality under Ivan I of the Rurik family, who made shrewd alliances, such as convincing leaders of the Orthodox Church to move their headquarters to Moscow in 1326. In 1480, Russia emerged as an independent country, under Ivan the Great. His son, Ivan IV, became king at age three. Although nobles, boyars, effectively ruled during his childhood, adult Ivan IV determined to modernize his country. He gave himself the title "czar," Russian for "caesar"; ordered the creation of a modern legal code; created trade alliances; conquered unclaimed lands; and spread settlements eastward. He created the oprichniks, a special police force which seized land from enemy boyars and executed political enemies, even Ivan's own family members. He ordered attacks on disobedient populations, such as the raid on Novgorod. Despite Ivan IV's harsh methods, Russia expanded and prospered economically under his rule. Thus his nickname, Ivan the Terrible, refers both to his fearsome violence and his awe-inspiring successes.

Romanovs

When Ivan the Terrible died in 1584 without an heir (because he had murdered his son), Russia went through a period of instability. Fyodor, the last heir of the Rurik Dynasty died in 1598, leaving no legitimate link to the previous monarchy. In the void, various nobles and officials vied for dominance, leading to widespread social disorder and uprisings. Numerous leaders rose and fell while other false leaders claimed popular support. Conflicts arose with Sweden and Poland, which invaded Russia in 1609. Without a strong czar who could unite the country, Russian leaders feared they would fall under foreign control. In 1613, the national assembly tried to restore order by naming Michael Romanov, a wealthy noble and distant relative of the Ruriks, as czar. Although only a teenager, Michael's presence helped unify the country. His relatives effectively ruled the country, but successfully restored order and created a strong new dynasty.

Bourbons

In 1537, Antoine de Bourbon, distant relative of the French Capetians, married Queen Jeanne of Navarre. By this time, the direct line of French Capetian monarchs had died out, replaced by the Valois family, which faced civil unrest between Huguenots and Catholics. Jeanne, a Calvinist, supported the Huguenots. As part of the French peace accord in 1570, Jeanne's son Henry married a member of the Valois family and converted to Catholicism. The French mistrusted Henry and held him at the palace for several years, even after he became king of Navarre upon his mother's death in 1572. Four years later he escaped, reaffirmed his Protestant commitment, and launched a new attack on French Catholics. Though that effort failed, it helped Henry build support for an attack on his Valois relatives when a succession crisis arose, popularly known as the War of the Three Henrys. Henry of Navarre was crowned king of France in 1589, establishing Bourbon rule.

Cardinal Richelieu

Cardinal Richelieu, a leader in the Catholic Church, was one of the most politically powerful men in France during the 1600s. When King Henry IV was murdered in 1610, his eight-year-old son, Louis XIII became king. Cardinal Richelieu became the king's chief minister in 1624. Because of ill health, Louis turned over most decision-making to Richelieu, a cunning politician who had a grand plan to

Copyright © Mometrix Media. You have been licensed one copy of this document for personal use only. Any other reproduction or redistribution is strictly prohibited. All rights reserved.
This content is provided for test preparation purposes only and does not imply an endorsement by Mometrix of any particular political, scientific, or religious point of view.

increase the power of the throne and thus the strength of France. Richelieu pushed through edicts to expand trade and manufacturing; weaken the political power of nobles, Huguenots, regional governors, and military leaders; and centralize government authority under the king. To achieve this last goal, Richelieu appointed intendants to oversee regional governments, reporting directly to the king. Richelieu also worked to encourage conflicts within other nations as a means of increasing France's power and influence. By the time Richelieu died in 1642, France was a powerful absolute monarchy.

Bloody Mary

Mary Tudor was the daughter of England's king and Catherine of Aragon. When Henry died in 1547, his only son, Edward VI, became king. The sickly boy died six years later without an heir. As the oldest of Henry's two daughters, Mary became the first reigning queen of England. However, Mary was a devout Catholic who opposed the Anglican Church her father had created. She married another ardent Catholic, Phillip II of Spain, who had led the Counter-Reformation in his country. Mary was determined to restore England to a Catholic nation and set out to thoroughly destroy the Anglican Church. She not only seized Anglican property and arrested its clergy, but also put hundreds of believers to death, many by public burning at the stake. Her actions backfired, igniting anger throughout England and increasing defense of the Church of England. By the time Mary died in 1558, she was widely vilified with the nickname "Bloody Mary."

Elizabeth I

When Mary I died without an heir, her half-sister, Elizabeth I, became queen. Elizabeth, the daughter of Henry VIII and Anne Boleyn, was a strong supporter of the Anglican Church and a popular figure among the people, to whom she reached out with a style uncommon among previous monarchs. Her image of devotion to duty, to the extent of never marrying, made her a revered figure akin to the Virgin Mary. Despite this popularity, during her early reign she faced constant threats from outside forces. Without an heir, Elizabeth's cousin, Mary Queen of Scots, would inherit the throne. The Catholic Mary conspired with Phillip II of Spain to depose Elizabeth and destroy the Anglican Church. When Mary fled to England to avoid a coup attempt, Elizabeth had her arrested. Upon discovering Mary's conspiracy with Phillip to assassinate her, Elizabeth ordered her cousin's execution in 1587. The conflict between Elizabeth and Phillip led their countries into war, but Elizabeth proved victorious, ushering in a golden age for England.

Elizabeth I's role in promoting Renaissance culture

Elizabeth I worked hard to cultivate a popular image of herself and a strong vision for her country. To that end, she recognized the value of utilizing the arts. As England's expanding markets increased public monies, Elizabeth became a strong supporter of the arts. Some of these artistic endeavors were sponsored to maintain her own image, such as the celebratory poems of Edmund Spenser (*The Faerie Queen*) and the royal portraits by Nicholas Hilliard. Other endeavors promoted the pride of English talent. Elizabeth I was a generous patron of the arts and encouraged the rise of popular theater, such as the plays of William Shakespeare and Christopher Marlowe. Moreover, Elizabeth promoted the expansion of literacy, so that by the time she died, England had one of the highest literacy rates in Europe.

James I

When Elizabeth I died without any children in 1603, her distant cousin, James I of Scotland, became king. James's ascension unified England and Scotland under one monarch. Although James was the son of the staunch Catholic Mary Queen of Scots, he was a strong defender of the Anglican Church. James ordered an English translation of the Bible. Written in a style similar to Shakespearean prose, the King James Bible became the predominant version for most Protestant denominations and is

Copyright © Mometrix Media. You have been licensed one copy of this document for personal use only. Any other reproduction or redistribution is strictly prohibited. All rights reserved.
This content is provided for test preparation purposes only and does not imply an endorsement by Mometrix of any particular political, scientific, or religious point of view.

still widely read today. Although pleased that he supported the Church of England, the English people never fully embraced the Scottish king as they had Elizabeth. James, a strong believer in absolute monarchy, often clashed with Parliament and members of the growing Puritan sect, who preferred a weak system of constitutional monarchy.

Gutenberg's printing press

Before the invention of the printing press, most literate Europeans read books which were carefully copied by hand. It took professional scribes a long time to copy a book. Although printing processes had existed among many different cultures for centuries, in 1450 German Johannes Gutenberg invented a new type of printing press which used movable type. The effect was revolutionary. Now multiple copies of books and other materials could be created in a fraction of the time it took to copy a text by hand. Printing presses quickly spread across Europe, putting many professional scribes out of business. Greater access to published works helped spread ideas and news more rapidly. Increased availability of books also piqued interest, encouraging the desire to read. As a result, education spread. Eventually, as more people learned to read, they challenged authority, such as by reading the Bible for themselves rather than relying solely upon priests' interpretations. Some citizens even became more outspoken about challenging church leaders and theology.

Change of education during the Renaissance

Prior to the Renaissance, education was primarily reserved for members of the nobility and clergy. Humanists encouraged expansion of education, including study in a wider diversity of fields as well as expansion of learning among the public. The rise of the printing press helped their beliefs become reality. With more printed materials available, more people became interested in learning to read. The Protestant Reformation led to an explosion of literacy education, since one of the movement's main goals was for followers to read the Bible and interpret it for themselves. Protestants encouraged education by creating schools. Luther encouraged parents to learn to read and then teach their children how to read. During the Counter Reformation, the Catholic Church responded by opening many new schools, including colleges and universities. The Jesuits led many of these educational efforts, encouraging learning while reinforcing traditional Catholic theology.

German conflict regarding indulgences

During the Renaissance, humanists encouraged questioning religious authority, especially abuses of authority that seemed at odds with true Christian theology. In many rising nations, powerful monarchs helped check abuses by church leaders. The German states, however, remained a loose confederation of old kingdoms, many led by weak princes. As a result, abuses of power by clergy became particularly concentrated in the German states. In 1517, Pope Leo X, seeking increased funds for the completion of St. Peter's Basilica, ordered monk Johann Tetzel to raise money in the northern German states. Tetzel's solution was to charge indulgences, payments followers made for the forgiveness of sins. The widespread charging of indulgences just to raise money outraged German humanists, who encouraged people to protest the practice.

Martin Luther and his protest against the Catholic Church

Martin Luther, a German monk from Saxony. questioned many church doctrines. Through intense study of the Bible, Luther came to develop several theories about faith which were at odds with contemporary Catholic practices. He believed that there was nothing humans could do to earn salvation or God's favor. Only true faith in God mattered. If people had true faith, he argued, they would model their behavior accordingly, but God only granted forgiveness based on belief. He called this theory "justification by grace through faith." Acting on these beliefs, in 1517 Luther strongly opposed Tetzel's indulgence policy as an unjust attempt to get people to buy their

Copyright © Mometrix Media. You have been licensed one copy of this document for personal use only. Any other reproduction or redistribution is strictly prohibited. All rights reserved.
This content is provided for test preparation purposes only and does not imply an endorsement by Mometrix of any particular political, scientific, or religious point of view.

salvation. As part of this protest, Luther nailed a list of 95 theses regarding indulgences on a church door in Wittenberg, Germany.

Protestant Reformation

Initially, Luther sought reform within the Catholic Church. Fearing widespread support for his position, church leaders denounced Luther. Rather than back down, he and his supporters increased their protests and expanded them beyond indulgences. Luther openly challenged church authority by claiming that the Bible, not clergy (even the Pope), should be the sole voice of religious authority. He expressed his beliefs that faith is more important than works, and God loves all believers equally. Luther used the power of the printing press to publish his ideas and distribute them throughout Europe. The pope excommunicated Luther, and then Holy Roman Emperor Charles V ordered his appearance before the Diet of Worms. When Luther refused to renounce his beliefs, Charles outlawed publication of his works (a widely ignored decree). Frederick the Wise, ruler of Saxony, protected Luther, enabling him to translate the first German version of the Bible. Luther's followers increased and came to call themselves "Protestants" because they were protesting Catholic policies. They eventually formed what would become Lutheranism.

Peace of Augsburg

The Protestant Reformation spread very quickly, especially in the German states, where several small sects arose to worship in their own way. Numerous German leaders embraced the movement and some princes made Lutheranism the official faith of their kingdoms in rejection of Catholicism. Holy Roman Emperor Charles V unsuccessfully tried to suppress the movement. In 1546, when diplomacy and threats failed, he sent troops into the Protestant German states. Despite losses on the battlefield, the Protestants refused to surrender. A beaten down Charles met with the princes in 1555 to establish the Peace of Augsburg. This treaty allowed each German state to choose its own religion. Residents opposed to the official faith would not be persecuted, but allowed to move. After the agreement was signed, most of the northern German states chose to become Protestant, further weakening Catholic power.

Anglican Church

In the midst of the Protestant Reformation brewing on the continent, England's King Henry VIII entered into a conflict with the pope over his desire for a divorce. Henry had been such a staunch Catholic and critic of Martin Luther that Pope Leo X had bestowed the title of "Defender of the Faith" upon him. Yet Henry was also obsessed with producing a male heir. His marriage to Catherine of Aragon had produced only a daughter, Mary (later "Bloody Mary"). In 1527, Henry decided to divorce Catherine to marry Anne Boleyn. When Pope Clement VII refused to grant the divorce, Henry responded by joining the Protestant movement and launching the Church of England (Anglican Church). The church initially retained most of the practices and ceremonies of the Catholic Church, substituting the British monarch for the pope as head of the church. In time, the Anglicans began to adopt more Protestant practices.

John Calvin

John Calvin was a French Protestant and follower of Swiss humanist theologian Huldrych Zwingli. Zwingli held many of the same beliefs as Luther, but promoted an even simpler approach to worship. After Zwingli was killed in a Catholic-Protestant battle, Calvin carried on his work, spelling out his theology in *The Institutes of Christian Religion* (1536). Calvin agreed with many of Luther's teachings, but they disagreed on several key points. Calvin promoted the idea of predestination, arguing that God had known since the beginning of time those who were destined for salvation. Those who were predestined were called the elect. Calvin said they could be identified by their high moral standards and self-discipline. As Calvinism spread, its followers established communities

Copyright © Mometrix Media. You have been licensed one copy of this document for personal use only. Any other reproduction or redistribution is strictly prohibited. All rights reserved.
This content is provided for test preparation purposes only and does not imply an endorsement by Mometrix of any particular political, scientific, or religious point of view.

which instituted strict practices and rigid rules to promote the self-discipline expected of the elect. The city of Geneva even adopted a government based on a Calvinist theocracy, leading some critics to argue that Calvinism was closer to Catholicism than Lutheranism.

Huguenots

The Huguenots were French Calvinists. The origin of the name Huguenots is unclear. Although France remained officially and in a majority of population a Catholic nation, French leaders viewed the Huguenots as a threat, largely because the faith was very popular among the lower classes. As such, the new faith represented a revolt against France's traditional class structure and political leadership which many closely associated the Catholic Church. For many years the Huguenots were persecuted by the government. In the latter 1500s, they fought numerous civil wars against French forces until King Henry IV's Edict of Nantes granted religious and some political freedom to the Huguenots. The wars resumed in the 1620s, resulting in the loss of Huguenot political power, though they were allowed to retain their faith.

Counter Reformation

The Counter Reformation, also called the Catholic Reformation, was a response to the spreading Protestant Movement. It took several different forms in various geographic regions. Pope Paul III is generally considered the founder of the Counter Reformation. When he became pope in 1534, Pope Paul III took Protestant concerns about church corruption very seriously, calling for a revival of spiritualism and high ethical standards among church leaders. He focused on appointing bishops and cardinals more concerned with faith than greed. In 1542, he launched the Roman Inquisition to suppress dissent within the church and called councils to clarify doctrine. Later popes expanded his efforts. In 1559, Pope Paul IV created the *Index of Forbidden Books* to suppress reading materials counter to church goals.

Council of Trent

This gathering of Catholic leaders emerged out of the Counter Reformation as a way of addressing unclear church doctrines and ending the types of corruption which had led to the Protestant Reformation. The council convened several times between 1545 and 1563. Some of their most important pronouncements included:

- Establishing the canon of Biblical books
- Fixing the seven church sacraments
- Affirming belief in original sin
- Establishing the miracle of the Eucharist through transubstantiation
- Establishing methods of completing penance
- Reaffirming that God only grant forgiveness through the priests of the church
- Declaring that salvation could be obtained through works as well as faith, counter to Protestant beliefs

Ignatius Loyola

During the Counter Reformation some religious orders were reorganized and some new ones emerged to reinforce new church doctrines. Spanish soldier and theologian Ignatius Loyola founded a priestly order called the Society of Jesus, or Jesuits, in 1534. He patterned the order after military units, with their focus on discipline and obedience, in which he had served. All Jesuits took vows of chastity, poverty, and obedience. Unlike monks, who usually lived in cloistered isolation, the Jesuits strove to actively serve in the world. They combined humanist philosophies with traditional Catholic doctrine in a way designed to counter the appeal of Protestantism. The Jesuit methods included embracing literacy and the educational movement. After Pope Paul III sanctified the order

Copyright © Mometrix Media. You have been licensed one copy of this document for personal use only. Any other reproduction or redistribution is strictly prohibited. All rights reserved.
This content is provided for test preparation purposes only and does not imply an endorsement by Mometrix of any particular political, scientific, or religious point of view.

in 1540, the Jesuits became the primary missionaries for the church, converting new members from eastern nations and slowing the spread of Protestantism in Europe.

Third Rome

The "third Rome" was Moscow. The title represents the city's central place in the Orthodox Church after the fall of Constantinople. During the Mongols' reign, the Russian branch of the Orthodox Church grew more independent from church leaders headquartered in Constantinople. In 1448, Russian bishops signaled a break with Constantinople by naming their own leader of the church to be headquartered in Moscow. Just five years later, Constantinople fell to the Ottomans, ending the Byzantine Empire. Afterwards, Moscow's church leaders declared their city the "third Rome," explaining that the first Rome (of the Roman Empire) and second Rome (Constantinople) had both fallen, leaving Moscow alone to represent the highest ideals of Orthodox Christianity. Church leaders reflected this position by constructing elaborate churches to inspire awe akin to the finest Catholic Cathedrals in Europe.

Witch hunts

The witch hunts represented an outbreak of efforts to identify people accused of occult activities. The efforts were often local in nature, but appeared throughout Europe, especially in the 1500s. Some were outgrowths of Inquisition attempts to ferret out heresy. Other cases represented reactions to social and economic uncertainties in changing times. Moreover, the witch hunts represented a widespread belief in superstition and magic. For most Europeans, the majority of whom remained illiterate, the world was an uncertain place. They believed that spirits, both good and bad, affected life on Earth and that humans could interpret the actions of the spirits or harness the spirits through occult observations and magic. Many of the accusations made in witch trials were based on gossip and exaggerated observations of harmless activities. They served as a way for ordinary people to gain power over others in a time of uncertainty and dramatic change. Although some scholars believed that citizens' increased education would weaken their belief in superstition, beliefs in witchcraft continued to be common even among learned people.

Copyright © Mometrix Media. You have been licensed one copy of this document for personal use only. Any other reproduction or redistribution is strictly prohibited. All rights reserved.
This content is provided for test preparation purposes only and does not imply an endorsement by Mometrix of any particular political, scientific, or religious point of view.

Practice Test

Want to take this practice test in an online interactive format?
Check out the online resources page, which includes interactive practice questions and much more: **mometrix.com/resources719/clepwescivi**

1. Which of the following is not a common characteristic of all early civilizations?

a. Agricultural surplus.
b. Clear division of labor.
c. A pictographic writing system.
d. Population centers such as towns and cities.
e. Some form of government.

2. Which of the following rivers did NOT play an important role in the development of the earliest civilizations?

a. The Tiber River.
b. The Yangtze River.
c. The Euphrates River.
d. The Nile River.
e. The Indus River.

3. "The river was easy to navigate because of a peculiar trait: Its strong winds blew in the opposite direction of its water's flow. The winds blew down from the north, but the river flowed up from the south. This unusual feature made it easy to transport goods back and forth from the Mediterranean Sea, which lay to the north.

Which river is most likely being described in the above passage?

a. The Tiber River.
b. The Tigris River.
c. The Nile River.
d. The Yangtze River.
e. The Indus River.

4. Which of the following rulers was female?

a. Sargon.
b. Hammurabi.
c. Hatshepsut.
d. Nebuchadnezzar.
e. Amenhotep IV.

Copyright © Mometrix Media. You have been licensed one copy of this document for personal use only. Any other reproduction or redistribution is strictly prohibited. All rights reserved.
This content is provided for test preparation purposes only and does not imply an endorsement by Mometrix of any particular political, scientific, or religious point of view.

5. "Because of the central role religion played in Sumerian culture, priests held much of the real power, despite the existence of a king. Beneath them a class of warrior nobles, responsible for protecting the city, held the next level of power. Less powerful than the nobles but still influential were the lower priests, scholars, and merchants who took responsibility for many of the daily operations of the government."

Which characteristic of most early civilizations does this passage reflect?

a. Agricultural surplus.
b. Population centers
c. Religious practice.
d. Development of technology
e. Government.

6. In what modern day country is the remains of Mesopotamian civilization found?

a. Afghanistan.
b. Iraq.
c. Turkey.
d. Egypt.
e. Lebanon.

7. "The king allowed the conquered the right to maintain their own religious practices, local laws, and customs. This practice, however, shares no similarities with our present-day principals of tolerance. In effect, allowing conquered people to maintain their own religions and customs forged a bond of loyalty between the conqueror and the conquered. Though the conquered preserved many rights and customs, local governors called Satraps, along with a network of spies, maintained order and reported back to the King."

Which empire does the above passage describe?

a. Persians.
b. Akkadians.
c. Babylonians.
d. Egyptians.
e. Sumerians.

8. A monotheistic religious practice was central to which of the following cultures?

a. Egyptians.
b. Hebrews.
c. Sumerians.
d. Babylonians.
e. Hittites.

9. Which of the following is a character from the *Epic of Gilgamesh*?

a. Ahura Mazda.
b. Enkidu.
c. Yahweh.
d. Thoth.
e. Zoroaster.

Copyright © Mometrix Media. You have been licensed one copy of this document for personal use only. Any other reproduction or redistribution is strictly prohibited. All rights reserved.
This content is provided for test preparation purposes only and does not imply an endorsement by Mometrix of any particular political, scientific, or religious point of view.

10. According to tradition, who founded the Israelite people?

a. Zoroaster.
b. Abraham.
c. Aeneas.
d. Daniel.
e. Jesus.

11. Which of the following was NOT developed by the Phoenicians?

a. Purple dye.
b. Sailing technology.
c. The alphabet.
d. Metalworking.
e. The ziggurat.

12. The first coin-based economy was established by which of the following people?

a. Phoenicians.
b. Egyptians.
c. Hebrews.
d. Lydians.
e. Babylonians.

13. Which of the following statements is NOT true of Minoan culture?

a. The name honors King Minos.
b. Its capital was in Knossos on the island of Crete.
c. Minoan culture was overtaken by the Athenians.
d. Its capital was a maze-like structure of many chambers.
e. Much of our knowledge of Minoan culture comes from reconstructed wall paintings.

14. The word democracy comes from two Greek root words meaning what?

a. People and rule.
b. People and vote.
c. City and state.
d. Tyrant and overthrow.
e. People and freedom.

15. Which of the following refers to the slave class of ancient Sparta?

a. Helots.
b. Hoplites.
c. Ephorate.
d. Metics.
e. Archon.

16. What was the Athenian Draco known for?

a. His severely punitive legal system.
b. His great reforms of the legal system.
c. Leading Athenians into defeat in Sicily.
d. Incurring the resentment of other city-states by amassing too much power.
e. His comedic plays.

Copyright © Mometrix Media. You have been licensed one copy of this document for personal use only. Any other reproduction or redistribution is strictly prohibited. All rights reserved.
This content is provided for test preparation purposes only and does not imply an endorsement by Mometrix of any particular political, scientific, or religious point of view.

17. Which of the following is not a significant event in the Persian Wars?

a. Persia invaded the Greek mainland.
b. Persians were driven back at the battle of Marathon.
c. The Greek forces vastly outnumbered the Persians.
d. The Persians attacked Athens.
e. Athens and Sparta unified their forces to defeat the Persians.

18. Which of the following is NOT an event associated with the golden age of Pericles?

a. Philosophy flourished under thinkers such as Socrates.
b. The Acropolis was reconstructed.
c. Many great plays were written and performed by tragedians such as Aeschylus and Sophocles.
d. The Iliad and Odyssey were written.
e. The study of history flourished under such historians as Herodotus and Thucydides.

19. Which of these factors did not contribute to the escalation of the Peloponnesian Wars?

a. Athens had amassed great power, which threatened other Greek city-states.
b. Athens had created a monopoly on sea trade in the region.
c. Several city-states formed an alliance with Sparta to keep Athens's power in check.
d. Athens invaded Sparta.
e. The Spartans invaded Attica, near Athens, in 431 B.C.

20. Which of the following statements are not true of BOTH the Iliad and the Odyssey?

a. Both deal with the Trojan War or its aftermaths.
b. Both focus primarily on the character Odysseus.
c. Both are attributed to a poet named Homer.
d. Both were written around 700 B.C.
e. Both were based on an oral tradition of bards reciting poems to audiences.

21. Who is the Greek goddess of war?

a. Aphrodite.
b. Hera.
c. Athena.
d. Demeter.
e. Artemis.

22. "In the 5th Century B.C., the most popular career choice for intelligent young Greek males was politics. To prepare children for life as a politician, many parents hired travelling teachers to instruct young pupils in such skills as rhetoric, politics, grammar, and history. The name for these educators derives from the Greek word for 'wisdom.'"

Who are the teachers described in the above passage?

a. Philosophers.
b. Sophists.
c. Rhetoricians.
d. Orators.
e. Politicians.

Copyright © Mometrix Media. You have been licensed one copy of this document for personal use only. Any other reproduction or redistribution is strictly prohibited. All rights reserved.
This content is provided for test preparation purposes only and does not imply an endorsement by Mometrix of any particular political, scientific, or religious point of view.

23. Which of the following statements about women in ancient Athens are not true?

a. Many female infants were abandoned or killed.
b. Women stayed in the home to manage servants and raise young children.
c. Women were allowed to vote, but their vote did not count as much as men's.
d. Women could not hold public office.
e. Women could not inherit property.

24. Which nation eventually overtook ancient Greece?

a. Persia.
b. Macedon.
c. Egypt.
d. Syria.
e. India.

25. Which of the following explanations accounts for the spread of Hellenism, i.e. Greek culture, in the decades following the overthrow of Greek power?

a. Many countries voluntarily adopted Greek government and culture because it was superior to their own.
b. Greek soldiers took control of the Persian Empire, imposing Greek culture on all of Persia's former conquests.
c. The spread of Hellenism was stopped after the overthrow of Greek power.
d. Rome was influenced by Greek culture and spread its version of Hellenism as it amassed power and territory.
e. Alexander, ruler of Macedon, adopted Greek culture as his own and spread it throughout the ancient world.

26. Which of the following statements are not true of Alexander the Great?

a. Alexander conquered Persia in 336 B.C.
b. Alexander took control of Egypt and founded Alexandria in 331 B.C.
c. Alexander conquered all of India.
d. Alexander's conquests ended after his troops mutinied.
e. Alexander died in 323 B.C. at the age of 33.

27. Which of the statements below is not true of the century following the death of Alexander?

a. Alexander's generals began fighting for control over the empire.
b. Alexander's brother took power only to be executed.
c. Alexander's heir took power and was executed.
d. Alexander's son brought peace to the empire and ushered in the Golden Age of Hellenistic Culture.
e. The generals divided the conquered lands into separate kingdoms and waged war with each other.

28. Which statement is closest to the core beliefs of the Greeks?

a. "Seize the day."
b. "Everything in moderation."
c. "Do unto others as you would have them do unto you."
d. "Live and let live."
e. "An eye for an eye."

Copyright © Mometrix Media. You have been licensed one copy of this document for personal use only. Any other reproduction or redistribution is strictly prohibited. All rights reserved.
This content is provided for test preparation purposes only and does not imply an endorsement by Mometrix of any particular political, scientific, or religious point of view.

29. Which of these statements does not reflect an influence on Greek art?

a. The symmetry of Greek sculpture and architecture shows the influence of geometry and mathematics.
b. Sculptures of bodies in motion show the Greek admiration of athletic skill.
c. The expressions of humility on the faces of statues reflect the belief that all humanity is fallen from grace.
d. The popularity of vases and pottery shows Greeks valued functionality as well as beauty.
e. The simple designs of Greek art reflect their distaste for excess and their praise of moderation.

30. Our primary source of knowledge about the philosophy of Socrates was preserved in what way?

a. On stone tablets he composed.
b. In the writings of his students.
c. On scrolls of papyrus he composed.
d. In comedic plays that depict his life.
e. In works written hundreds of years after his death.

31. "This school of thought held that certainty is an illusion because no knowledge can be absolutely true. The universe constantly changes, and what is true for one time is not true for all. Thinkers who followed this school's founder, Pyrrho, questioned all scientific and religious beliefs."

The above passage reflects which of the following school of thought?

a. Skepticism.
b. Epicureanism.
c. Cynicism.
d. Stoicism.
e. Dualism.

32. "They are indestructible, constantly in motion, indivisible, and infinite. All material substances are composed of them. This theory of atoms is remarkable in that it anticipates scientific theories that would be confirmed two and a half millennia later."

Which of the following Greek philosophers is primarily responsible for the ideas described in the above passage?

a. Socrates.
b. Aristotle.
c. Plato.
d. Thales.
e. Democritus.

Copyright © Mometrix Media. You have been licensed one copy of this document for personal use only. Any other reproduction or redistribution is strictly prohibited. All rights reserved.
This content is provided for test preparation purposes only and does not imply an endorsement by Mometrix of any particular political, scientific, or religious point of view.

33. Which of the following statements about Greek contribution to modern science is not true?

a. Aristotle was one of the first to explore the fields we now know as comparative anatomy, taxonomy, and embryology.
b. Socrates was the first to argue that the material world is composed of indivisible units called atoms.
c. Hippocrates separated the study of medicine from religion and was one of the first to establish effective medical theories.
d. Herophilus dissected cadavers to advance the field of human anatomy.
e. Euclid established many of the foundations of the study of geometry.

34. The three works by Aeschylus, *Agamemnon, Libation Bearers,* and *Eumenides* make up the only surviving trilogy of Greek drama known as

a. The Oresteia.
b. The Oedipus Trilogy.
c. The Iliad.
d. The Odyssey.
e. The Antigone Trilogy.

35. Which of the following events was the central focus of Herodotus' work, The *Histories*?

a. The Persian invasion of the Greek mainland.
b. The infiltration of Troy by soldiers hidden in a wooden horse.
c. Sparta's defeat of Athens.
d. King Oedipus' realization that he had married his own mother.
e. The murder of Agamemnon.

36. "He was one of Socrates' star pupils who went on to found the Academy in Athens to teach philosophy. He preferred to express his ideas in dramatic dialog, a style that often makes it hard to determine the exact point of view he promoted. Among his best known arguments is the theory of forms, which argues that the world we experience is an imperfect reflection of a higher, idealized realm."

The above passage refers to which famous Greek philosopher?

a. Aristotle.
b. Thales.
c. Anaxagoras.
d. Parmenides.
e. Plato.

37. Which of the following statements about the education of wealthy Athenian males is false?

a. Children attended group schools where they studied reading, writing, poetry, and grammar.
b. Children were taken out of their homes and placed in a grueling public education program designed to build physical and psychological endurance.
c. Children studied sports such as gymnastics, javelin throwing, and boxing.
d. Adolescents studied government, ethics, mathematics, and rhetoric in the schools of the Sophists.
e. Eighteen-year olds were obligated to spend one year in military service.

Copyright © Mometrix Media. You have been licensed one copy of this document for personal use only. Any other reproduction or redistribution is strictly prohibited. All rights reserved.
This content is provided for test preparation purposes only and does not imply an endorsement by Mometrix of any particular political, scientific, or religious point of view.

38. Which group overtook Rome in the mid-600s BC and established much of its infrastructure, including sewers, roads, and fortifications, only to be driven out of the city in 509 BC?

a. Latins.
b. Etruscans.
c. Greeks.
d. Persians.
e. Mesopotamians.

39. Which of the following facts about the Latins is false?

a. Their culture was influenced by southern Italian tribes.
b. They established their first villages along the Tiber River.
c. They united to create the city of Rome around 300 A.D.
d. Their language became the language of the Roman Empire.
e. They took the city again after it had been occupied and rebuilt by a kingdom from the north.

40. "These men occupied the most powerful level of the Roman Republic. They were responsible for controlling the public treasury and foreign policy. Once appointed, they held the position for the remainder of their lives. They were even entitled to appoint a dictator for a six-month period in the event of an emergency."

Who does the above passage describe?

a. Senators.
b. Magistrates.
c. Praetors.
d. Censors.
e. Consuls.

41. Which of the following is not an effect of the Punic Wars between Rome and Carthage?

a. Over the course of the wars, Rome developed a powerful navy.
b. After suffering defeat in all three of the Punic Wars, Carthage was destroyed.
c. Rome emerged as the dominant power in the Mediterranean.
d. Carthage emerged more powerful than before the Punic Wars, becoming a serious threat to Roman power.
e. Macedonia lost its influence in the region.

42. The Conflict of the Orders was a dispute between

a. Rome and Carthage.
b. Rome and Macedonia.
c. The Latins, Greeks, and Etruscans.
d. Wealthy Roman landowners and the lower class Plebeians.
e. Rome and Sicily.

43. What caused the first Punic War in 246 B.C.?

a. Hannibal attacked Rome from the mountainous north.
b. The Romans destroyed Carthage and sold all its citizens into slavery.
c. Carthage intervened in a dispute between Rome and the island of Sicily.
d. Rome defeated Macedonia.
e. Roman forces attacked northern Africa.

Copyright © Mometrix Media. You have been licensed one copy of this document for personal use only. Any other reproduction or redistribution is strictly prohibited. All rights reserved.
This content is provided for test preparation purposes only and does not imply an endorsement by Mometrix of any particular political, scientific, or religious point of view.

44. What was the main reason Julius Caesar was assassinated in 44 B.C.?

a. He had removed himself to the Island of Capri to lead a life of depravity.
b. His political opponents believed he had amassed too much power.
c. He appointed his horse to the senate.
d. He led his armies in an attack against Rome.
e. He and Cleopatra attempted to attack Augustus at the Battle of Actium.

45. Who was not a member of the Julio-Claudian line of Roman Emperors?

a. Tiberius.
b. Claudius.
c. Caligula.
d. Nero.
e. Marcus Aurelius.

46. The "Good Emperors" who ruled Rome from 96 to 180 A.D. included:

a. Nerva, Trajan, Hadrian, Antoninus Pius, and Marcus Aurelius.
b. Tiberius Gracchus, Gaius Gracchus, Gaius Marius, and Lucius Cornelius Sulla.
c. Galba, Otho, and Vitellius.
d. Pertinax, Didius Julianus, Septimius Serverus, Pescennius Niger, and Clodius Albinus.
e. Augustus, Tiberius, Caligula, Claudius, and Nero.

47. "This era represents the golden age of the Roman Empire. For about 200 years, the Empire experienced relatively few attacks, stability among its conquered lands, and significant developments in architecture and the engineering of roads and bridges. This time period saw the greatest expansion of the empire and the Romanization of the western world."

The above passage refers to which era of Roman history?

a. The reign of Julio-Claudian line of emperors.
b. The reign of the Five Good Emperors.
c. Pax Romana.
d. The reign of the Flavian Emperors.
e. The era of the Gracchi.

48. Which of the following is not a major structure found in the city of Rome?

a. The Forum.
b. The Pantheon.
c. Hadrian's Wall.
d. The Colosseum.
e. House of the Vestal Virgins.

49. Led by Spartacus, the revolt in 73-71 B.C. reflects the disgruntlement of

a. The Praetorian Guard.
b. Senators.
c. Slaves.
d. Centuria.
e. The conquered provinces.

Copyright © Mometrix Media. You have been licensed one copy of this document for personal use only. Any other reproduction or redistribution is strictly prohibited. All rights reserved.
This content is provided for test preparation purposes only and does not imply an endorsement by Mometrix of any particular political, scientific, or religious point of view.

50. Which of the following did not make a significant contribution to Roman literature?

a. Horace.
b. Livy.
c. Plutarch.
d. Homer.
e. Virgil.

51. What did The *Metamorphoses* by the Roman poet Ovid describe?

a. The history of Greece.
b. The history of the Roman Republic.
c. Greek and Roman Myths.
d. The poet's advice for lovers.
e. The poet's family history.

52. To what do many historians attribute the Romans' preoccupation with bloodthirsty forms of entertainment such as gladiator battles and public executions?

a. High standard of living.
b. Pagan religious practices.
c. Moral decline.
d. Stoicism.
e. Economic decline.

53. "Before his religious conversion, he persecuted Jews who converted to Christianity. After experiencing a religious vision, he became the early Christian church's strongest proponent, founding and counseling churches throughout Greece and Macedonia. These churches went on to form the foundation of the religion that would eventually spread throughout the Roman Empire."

The above passage describes which of the men shown below?

a. Jesus.
b. Paul.
c. Peter.
d. David.
e. John.

54. Which of the following emperors made Christianity the official religion of the Roman Empire?

a. Theodosius.
b. Nero.
c. Marcus Aurelius.
d. Julius Caesar.
e. Hadrian.

55. Which of the following groups did not play a role in the Germanic invasions of Rome?

a. Ostrogoths.
b. Visigoths.
c. Vandals.
d. Huns.
e. Etruscans.

Copyright © Mometrix Media. You have been licensed one copy of this document for personal use only. Any other reproduction or redistribution is strictly prohibited. All rights reserved.
This content is provided for test preparation purposes only and does not imply an endorsement by Mometrix of any particular political, scientific, or religious point of view.

56. Which of the following factors did not lead to the split between the eastern and western Roman Empires?

a. Diocletian's decision to split the empire into two separate centers with authority divided between himself and a co-emperor.
b. Corruption and instability in the government.
c. The onset of the Crusades, a war between the eastern and western branches of the Christian Church.
d. Constantinople's emergence as a powerful city.
e. A widening gap between wealthy and impoverished citizens.

57. Which of the following statements does NOT describe Rome's relationship with its conquered peoples?

a. All subjects were granted the full range of rights entitled to Roman citizens.
b. The Romans allowed some degree of cultural autonomy.
c. Subjects were expected to follow Roman laws.
d. Subjects were obligated to pay taxes.
e. Subjects gave up land and supplies to the government.

58. In the 500s A.D., Byzantine emperor Justinian compiled the Justinian Code. What does this code contain?

a. Roman laws and legal opinions.
b. The history of the Roman Emperors.
c. Roman religious practice.
d. Roman economic policies.
e. The great works of Roman literature.

59. What did the Iconoclasts oppose?

a. The elevation of religious leaders to powerful positions.
b. The use of religious images in worship.
c. The worship of saints.
d. The worship of the Mother Mary.
e. The watering-down of Christianity for the illiterate.

60. Which of the following is not one of the five pillars of Islam?

a. The profession of faith, "There is no god but Allah; Muhammad is the prophet of Allah."
b. The ritual of five daily prayers.
c. Payments made to provide for the poor and needy within a community.
d. One pilgrimage to holy city of Mecca in the Muslim's lifetime.
e. Abstinence from eating unclean animals.

61. This title meant "successor to the prophet" and was given to the main Islamic leaders who came to power after Mohammad's death.

a. Imam.
b. Caliph.
c. Sultan.
d. Sheik.
e. Vizier.

Copyright © Mometrix Media. You have been licensed one copy of this document for personal use only. Any other reproduction or redistribution is strictly prohibited. All rights reserved.
This content is provided for test preparation purposes only and does not imply an endorsement by Mometrix of any particular political, scientific, or religious point of view.

62. Which of the following scientific contributions was not made by Arabic thinkers?

a. The development of the Arabic numbering system.
b. The development of algebra.
c. Significant advances in trigonometry.
d. The invention of the abacus.
e. Advances in the use of decimals.

63. Which of the following events did not happen between 500 and 1000 A.D., the period known as the "Dark Ages"?

a. The fall of the Roman Empire.
b. The fragmentation of areas formally unified by Roman rule.
c. Cultural isolation due to the loss of dependable trade routes.
d. The global collapse of civilization.
e. Europe's loss of much of the knowledge advanced by Greek and Roman thinkers.

64. "His accomplishments include defeating the Lombards, Saxons, and Avars throughout Europe, deterring advances by Muslim armies in the Pyrenees Mountains, reviving Roman legal practice, increasing the strength of the Roman Catholic church, becoming the first Holy Roman Emperor of Europe, and establishing schools and libraries throughout Europe."

Who does the above passage describe?

a. Charlemagne.
b. Pope Leo III.
c. Charles Martel.
d. Clovis I.
e. Pepin II.

65. Under feudalism, this term refers to a person who controlled a large landholding and gave parts of it away in exchange for loyalty and protection.

a. Fief.
b. Homage.
c. Lord.
d. Primogeniture.
e. Vassal.

66. Which of the following statements is not true of manorialism?

a. The lord of a manor gave his land to serfs to cultivate.
b. The serfs kept just enough of the crops to sustain themselves but gave the majority to the lord.
c. Many serfs who worked diligently could become nobles.
d. Nobles lived apart from the serfs in a castle complex.
e. The serfs gave crops to the nobles in exchange for protection.

67. Which of the following statements is not true of the hierarchy of the Catholic Church?

a. Parish priests made up a diocese.
b. The head of the diocese was called a bishop.
c. The archdiocese was a collection of smaller dioceses overseen by the archbishop.
d. The curia was a group of archbishops with power over the pope.
e. The pope is the ultimate authority for the church.

Copyright © Mometrix Media. You have been licensed one copy of this document for personal use only. Any other reproduction or redistribution is strictly prohibited. All rights reserved.
This content is provided for test preparation purposes only and does not imply an endorsement by Mometrix of any particular political, scientific, or religious point of view.

68. Which of the following terms describes the practice of abolishing Catholics who did not believe in official church policies or doctrines?

a. Heretics.
b. Excommunication.
c. Interdict.
d. Canon Law.
e. Indulgences.

69. Which of the following held themselves to the code of chivalry?

a. Serfs.
b. Archbishops.
c. Troubadours.
d. Vassals.
e. Knights.

70. Which of the following statements best characterizes the work of Thomas Aquinas?

a. He attempted to use the logical techniques developed by Aristotle to justify belief in the divinity of Christ.
b. His Canterbury Tales was written in a vernacular language instead of Latin.
c. His Divine Comedy tells the story of a man's journey into hell, through purgatory, and onward to paradise.
d. His followers, the Franciscans, attempted to follow in the footsteps of Jesus, travelling and ministering while refusing financial compensation.
e. He believed that the church was like a "city of God" separate from the "city of man."

71. This organization helped protect the rights of workers who practiced a craft.

a. Charters.
b. Fief.
c. Manor.
d. Guilds.
e. Banks.

72. To what does the term "Black Death" refer?

a. Viking warfare in the 9th Century.
b. The plague that killed 25 million in the 1300s.
c. An execution method common in the feudal system.
d. Excommunication by the Catholic Church.
e. A form of combat used among knights.

73. Who were the Angles and Saxons?

a. Viking invaders of England.
b. Groups from French Normandy.
c. Members of the emerging middle class.
d. Merchants who travelled European trade routes.
e. Two of the many Germanic groups who competed for dominance after the fall of Rome.

Copyright © Mometrix Media. You have been licensed one copy of this document for personal use only. Any other reproduction or redistribution is strictly prohibited. All rights reserved.
This content is provided for test preparation purposes only and does not imply an endorsement by Mometrix of any particular political, scientific, or religious point of view.

74. Which of the following events did not take place in the year 1066?

a. The heirless king of the Anglo-Saxons, Edward the Confessor, died.
b. Harold of Wessex was chosen as Edward's successor.
c. William the Conqueror led forces across the English Channel to battle Harold's forces at the Battle of Hastings.
d. The English army mutinied to avoid battle, granting William power without bloodshed.
e. William brought the customs of monarchial feudalism to England.

75. Which of the following statements is not true of the Magna Carta?

a. In 1215, powerful nobles almost overthrew King John, who signed the Magna Carta in order to stay in power.
b. It took away nearly all of the powers of the monarchy.
c. The term means "Great Charter."
d. It held monarchs to the same laws as others.
e. It provided many rights to citizens.

76. A French peasant girl, Joan of Arc, had visions from the saints. What did they tell her to do?

a. Lead French troops to attack the English.
b. Lead troops to retake control of Jerusalem.
c. Become the first female priest in the Catholic Church.
d. Overthrow Charles VII of France.
e. To lead the Children's Crusade.

77. Which of the following is not a cause of the first Crusade?

a. The Turks overtook Jerusalem in 1065.
b. 3,000 Christian pilgrims were massacred in Jerusalem.
c. Turks threatened to invade Constantinople.
d. Pope Urban II argued that defense of Jerusalem was a Christian obligation, sparking a holy war.
e. To distract the public from the abuse of power seen during the Inquisition.

78. Launched in the late 1200s, the Inquisition attempted to

a. Identify heretics and undermine the growing threat of Christian sects.
b. Inspire a holy war against Muslims.
c. Unite the eastern and western branches of the Catholic Church.
d. To resolve the tensions between the church and the kings of European nation-states.
e. Root out abuses of power in the Catholic Church.

79. Which of the following statements does not describe the Great Schism?

a. Several powerful kings began to contest the authority of the Church.
b. King Philip IV of France used his political influence to install a pope whom he could control.
c. The Eastern Orthodox Church and the Roman Catholic Church separated.
d. The pope was moved from Italy to Avignon, France.
e. Different political factions each instated their own popes, with as many as three popes ruling at once.

Copyright © Mometrix Media. You have been licensed one copy of this document for personal use only. Any other reproduction or redistribution is strictly prohibited. All rights reserved.
This content is provided for test preparation purposes only and does not imply an endorsement by Mometrix of any particular political, scientific, or religious point of view.

80. "In 1207, he decided to abandon all of his material possessions and devote himself to serve God. Soon, many followed his path and committed themselves to a life of poverty and service to the poor in an attempt to emulate the life of Jesus."

Who is the person described in this passage?

a. John Wycliffe.
b. Jan Hus.
c. St. Francis of Assisi.
d. Pope Leo III.
e. Martin Luther.

81. "As the Crusades opened up new trade routes to the East, they also forged stronger bonds between Europe and the Byzantine Empire, which had preserved many of the great works of Greek and Roman science. As a result, Europe's interest in philosophy and science was rekindled, and a period of rapid intellectual advancement began."

What is the era described in this passage is known as?

a. The Reformation.
b. Middle Ages.
c. The Renaissance.
d. The Counter Reformation.
e. The Scientific Revolution.

82. Members of this wealthy family were famous for financing many great works by Italian artists in the 15th Century. They were known as patrons.

a. The Medici.
b. The Machiavelli.
c. The Ghiberti.
d. The Brunischelli.
e. The Botticelli.

83. The 15th Century produced many influential artists in Florence, Italy whose work shaped much of what would become recognized as Renaissance art. Which of the following was not an artist from Florence?

a. Filippo Brunelleschi.
b. Masaccio.
c. Lorenzo Ghiberti.
d. Sandro Botticelli.
e. Erasmus.

84. "This school of thought first emerged in the 1300s among Europeans who studied ancient Greek and Roman grammar, history, poetry, and rhetoric. They believed strongly in human dignity, looked for common bonds between different religions and philosophies, and strove for a civilization that would be enriched by learning."

What is the school of thought described in this paragraph?

a. Humanism.
b. Scholasticism.
c. Philosophy.
d. Syncretism.
e. Classicism.

Copyright © Mometrix Media. You have been licensed one copy of this document for personal use only. Any other reproduction or redistribution is strictly prohibited. All rights reserved.
This content is provided for test preparation purposes only and does not imply an endorsement by Mometrix of any particular political, scientific, or religious point of view.

85. Which of the following is not a major work by Michelangelo?

a. Frescoes on the ceiling of the Sistine Chapel.
b. Pieta.
c. David.
d. The Last Judgment.
e. Mona Lisa.

86. Leonardo Da Vinci made important contributions to engineering, architecture, painting, sculpture, and science. Which of the following terms best describes him?

a. Reformist.
b. Renaissance Man.
c. Humanist.
d. Artist.
e. Realist.

87. The country of Flanders produced many masters of the medium of oil painting, known as the Flemish School. Which of the following is not a member of the Flemish school?

a. Jan van Eyck.
b. Hubert van Eyck.
c. Pieter Brueghel.
d. Gerard David.
e. Raphael.

88. Which English humanist authored *Utopia?*

a. Erasmus.
b. William Shakespeare.
c. Albrecht Durer.
d. Thomas More.
c. John Milton.

89. "He became king at the age of three, and as an adult he committed himself to the modernization of his country. He gave himself the title 'czar' (which is the Russian word for 'Caesar': created a modern legal code, forged strong trade alliances, and conquered a vast territory for Russia. Though he saw his country through significant progress, he was also ruthless in persecuting those he saw as political enemies, including his own son."
Who is the Russian king described in this passage?

a. Ivan the Terrible.
b. Michael Romanov.
c. Genghis Khan.
d. Ivan the Great.
e. Ivan I.

90. Which of the following kingdoms was not part of the unification of the Iberian Peninsula now known as Spain?

a. Aragon.
b. Castile.
c. Granada.
d. Kiev.
e. Navarre.

Copyright © Mometrix Media. You have been licensed one copy of this document for personal use only. Any other reproduction or redistribution is strictly prohibited. All rights reserved.
This content is provided for test preparation purposes only and does not imply an endorsement by Mometrix of any particular political, scientific, or religious point of view.

91. Why did Henry VIII's daughter, Mary Tudor, earn the nickname "Bloody Mary"?

a. She violently drove the Moors from her country.
b. She declared war against France.
c. She persecuted members of the Anglican Church.
d. She refused to grant the king a divorce.
e. She persecuted Catholics.

92. To what does the term "indulgence" refer?

a. Priests granting a reduction of punishment for sins.
b. Political pardons offered by kings.
c. Commissions for portraits.
d. Patronizing or financing artists.
e. Excessive imagery in Renaissance art.

93. Which of the following is not a byproduct of the invention of the printing press?

a. A challenge to church authority because people could read the Bible for themselves.
b. An increase in literacy.
c. The Great Schism, a period when the authority of the church was separated between multiple popes.
d. The rapid spread of ideas.
e. The spread of education.

94. Which of the following is not a core belief of Martin Luther?

a. Individuals should read the Bible for themselves.
b. Priests should charge money for the forgiveness of sins.
c. Humans cannot earn salvation by good deeds alone.
d. True faith in God matters above all else.
e. A fee for indulgences was wrong.

95. What is the main reason King Henry VIII started the Anglican Church?

a. He was an advocate of Martin Luther.
b. The pope refused to grant him a divorce.
c. He wished to become pope.
d. He wished to rule over all Catholics.
e. He questioned the divinity of Jesus.

96. "Her strong support of the Anglican Church, her devotion to her role as Queen—to the extent of never marrying—and her generous patronage of popular arts all helped establish her as a popular and beloved Queen. Despite her popularity among her subjects, England was under threat for much of her reign. She uncovered an assassination plot led by her cousin, Mary Queen of Scots, and Phillip II of Spain, which in part brought about war between England and Spain."

Who is the queen described in this passage?

a. Elizabeth I.
b. Anne Boleyn.
c. Mary Tudor.
d. Catherine of Aragon.
e. Isabella.

Copyright © Mometrix Media. You have been licensed one copy of this document for personal use only. Any other reproduction or redistribution is strictly prohibited. All rights reserved.
This content is provided for test preparation purposes only and does not imply an endorsement by Mometrix of any particular political, scientific, or religious point of view.

97. Which of the following reflects a point of disagreement between the theologies of John Calvin and Martin Luther?

a. Jesus' divinity.
b. The trinity of God the Father, God the Son, and God the Holy Spirit.
c. The doctrine of the Eucharist.
d. The reform of the Catholic Church.
e. Justification by faith alone.

98. Which of the following statements is not true of the Counter Reformation?

a. It was founded by Pope Paul III.
b. The pope responded to Protestant criticisms of the Catholic Church.
c. It called for a return to spirituality and ethics among the church leadership.
d. It called for a war against Protestants.
e. It called for assemblies to clarify church doctrine.

99. Which of the following is not true of the Council of Trent?

a. It established the official canon of Biblical books.
b. It ruled that one could only receive forgiveness through priests.
c. It declared that salvation could be gained through good deeds as well as faith.
d. It renounced the doctrine of original sin.
e. It established the methods of penance for one's sins.

100. Who is the Italian writer whose book *The Prince* made his name synonymous with duplicity and dishonesty?

a. Francesco Petrarch.
b. Baldassare Castiglione.
c. Filippo Brunelleschi.
d. Sandro Botticelli.
e. Niccolo Machiavelli.

101. Which of the following cities was known as the "Third Rome"?

a. Kiev.
b. Moscow.
c. London.
d. Paris.
e. Constantinople.

102. Who was not an early explorer of the Americas?

a. Amerigo Vespucci.
b. Ferdinand Magellan.
c. John Cabot.
d. Henry Hudson.
e. Ignatius Loyola.

Copyright © Mometrix Media. You have been licensed one copy of this document for personal use only. Any other reproduction or redistribution is strictly prohibited. All rights reserved.
This content is provided for test preparation purposes only and does not imply an endorsement by Mometrix of any particular political, scientific, or religious point of view.

103. Which of the following statements is not true of the rash of witch hunts that took place in the 14th through 16th centuries in Europe?

a. The witch hunts used the Inquisition's techniques for rooting out heretics.
b. Many hunts followed careful legal codes.
c. Much of the evidence used was based on hearsay.
d. Belief in magic and superstition was commonplace even among educated Europeans.
e. It is estimated that between 40,000 and 100,000 suspected witches were killed during the Early Modern period.

104. Which of the following technological advancements did not lead to increased sea travel?

a. Improvements in mapmaking.
b. Improvements in the compass.
c. The invention of the astrolabe.
d. Improvements in shipbuilding.
e. Development of the steam engine.

105. Which of the following is not a reason why Europeans began colonizing other lands?

a. They wanted to Christianize other peoples they viewed as savages.
b. Drought, famine, and war had destroyed most of Europe.
c. They needed to find additional sources of silver and gold to coin money.
d. They could establish new markets for goods produced in Europe.
e. They could reduce overpopulation in the home country by sending colonists to new regions.

106. Which of the following is not part of triangular trade?

a. Sailing from Europe to Africa.
b. Trading goods for slaves.
c. Selling the slaves to plantation owners in the Americas.
d. Trading American goods in Asia.
e. Selling American goods in Europe.

107. Which American city did the Dutch East India Company purchase in 1626 and name New Amsterdam?

a. Charleston.
b. New York City.
c. New Orleans.
d. Boston.
e. Philadelphia.

108. Why did enmity and hostility grow between Spain and England in the late 1500s?

a. The creation of the Anglican Church angered Catholic Spain.
b. Members of British royalty conspired to assassinate the Spanish king.
c. England had supported Turkish invaders who attempted to attack Spain in the early 1500s.
d. Spain financed pirate attacks on English vessels.
e. Spain supported an anti-English uprising in the Netherlands.

Copyright © Mometrix Media. You have been licensed one copy of this document for personal use only. Any other reproduction or redistribution is strictly prohibited. All rights reserved.
This content is provided for test preparation purposes only and does not imply an endorsement by Mometrix of any particular political, scientific, or religious point of view.

109. In what region did the Thirty Years' War take place?

a. Eastern Europe.
b. The British Isles.
c. Spain.
d. France.
e. Italy.

110. To what does the "long Parliament" refer?

a. A period when King James I clashed with Parliament because they denied his requests to raise taxes.
b. An eleven-year period when King Charles refused to allow Parliament to convene except when absolutely necessary.
c. Queen Elizabeth's reign, because she rarely called the Parliament into session.
d. A period when Parliament opposed English sea trade, which limited competition with other countries pursuing colonization.
e. The period when Parliament attempted to oppose the creation of the Anglican Church.

111. Even though Elizabeth I claimed they were renegades over whom she had no control, what were the seadogs financed by the British to do?

a. Spy on rival governments.
b. Attack the ships of rivals at sea.
c. Smuggle illegal trade items.
d. Assassinate political enemies.
e. Sabotage rival countries' colonies abroad.

112. Which of the following factors did not contribute to Spain's decline as a global power in the 16th Century?

a. England's defeat of the Spanish Armada in 1588.
b. A failed invasion of France.
c. A huge trade deficit.
d. Invasions by Moors who overtook much of the region.
e. The Reconquista, an attempt to drive all non-Catholics out of Spain, which effectively cost Spain all of their talents and innovations.

113. The Cavaliers and Roundheads were warring factions in what event?

a. The English Civil War.
b. The Long Parliament.
c. The Thirty Years War.
d. The Reformation.
e. The Netherlands' rebellion against Spain.

114. What did the Scientific Revolution emphasize?

a. Tradition and authority.
b. Observation and reason.
c. Superstition.
d. Theology.
e. Mythology.

Copyright © Mometrix Media. You have been licensed one copy of this document for personal use only. Any other reproduction or redistribution is strictly prohibited. All rights reserved.
This content is provided for test preparation purposes only and does not imply an endorsement by Mometrix of any particular political, scientific, or religious point of view.

115. Who is the author of *Dialogue Concerning the Two Chief World Systems, Ptolemaic and Copernican* that argued the Earth was not the center of the universe?

a. Copernicus.
b. Galileo Galilei.
c. Johannes Kepler.
d. Rene Descartes.
e. Francis Bacon.

116. This medical scientist was the first to describe how blood cycles throughout the veins and heart.

a. Francis Bacon.
b. Roger Bacon.
c. William Harvey.
d. Ambroise Paré.
e. Andreas Vesalius.

117. Which of the following does not reflect a basic belief of the Puritans?

a. They believed the Anglican Church had lost touch with the best aspects of the Catholic tradition.
b. They believed the elect are predestined to salvation.
c. Their theology was closer to Calvinism than to Anglicanism.
d. They wanted to purify the Anglican Church and remove all remnants of Catholicism.
e. They believed individuals should have a personal religious experience.

118. "The first English settlement in North America, this town was primarily established as an economic venture. The colonists who arrived in the region in 1607 had been sent there for financial purposes, not necessarily for the religious freedoms that motivated later settlements. Several years passed before it turned its first profit with a tobacco crop in 1614, and the years between its settlement and its first economic successes were a period of lawlessness and starvation for many of the settlers."

What is the town described in this passage?

a. Plymouth.
b. Jamestown.
c. Charleston.
d. St. Augustine.
e. Salem.

119. Which of the following statements is not true of daily life for the average European in the 1500s?

a. Life was not significantly different from the medieval era.
b. The majority of people worked in agriculture.
c. Life expectancy was short.
d. Most people were literate, due to well-financed public education programs.
e. The Commercial Revolution and the colonization of new lands made new opportunities possible for the first time.

Copyright © Mometrix Media. You have been licensed one copy of this document for personal use only. Any other reproduction or redistribution is strictly prohibited. All rights reserved.
This content is provided for test preparation purposes only and does not imply an endorsement by Mometrix of any particular political, scientific, or religious point of view.

120. Which of the following statements does not describe the average European diet BEFORE the expansion of trade routes?

a. Europeans ate for survival, not enjoyment.
b. They had an abundance of preservatives such as salt that could make food last longer.
c. Grain-based foods such as porridge and bread were staple meals.
d. Spices were unavailable.
e. Luxury items such as tea, sugar, and coffee had not yet been introduced.

Copyright © Mometrix Media. You have been licensed one copy of this document for personal use only. Any other reproduction or redistribution is strictly prohibited. All rights reserved.
This content is provided for test preparation purposes only and does not imply an endorsement by Mometrix of any particular political, scientific, or religious point of view.

Answers and Explanations

1. C: Though Egypt had a well-known pictographic writing system called hieroglyphs, other cultures used different forms of writing. For example, cuneiform is a language that does not use pictographs. The remaining choices played an essential role in all early civilizations.

2. A: Roman civilization developed on the Tiber River, but it is not considered one of the earliest civilizations. Major civilizations developed along the other rivers listed: Chinese civilization developed in the Yangtze and Huang River valleys; Mesopotamian civilization emerged between the Tigris and Euphrates; and Egyptian culture developed in the Nile River valley.

3. C: This passage contains two clues to the answer: one the river flows north and two the river lies to the south of the Mediterranean Sea. The Nile is the only river listed that flows south-to-north and lies to the south of the Mediterranean, making *C* the best choice. These geographical clues can be used to exclude the other choices: the Tiber is incorrect because it lies to the north of the Mediterranean Sea. The other choices are incorrect because these rivers lie east or southeast of the sea.

4. C: Hatshepsut was an Egyptian Pharaoh whose name means "foremost of noble ladies." Sargon, Hammurabi, Nebuchadnezzar, and Amenhotep IV were men.

5. E: This passage details the political hierarchy of the Sumerian government. Little mention is made of agricultural surplus, population centers, or technology. *C* is incorrect because the passage primarily focuses on the structure of Sumerian government.

6. B: Mesopotamian civilization developed in the Tigris and Euphrates River Valley, an area now controlled by Iraq. None of the other answers accurately reflects the geography of the region.

7. A: The word "Satrap" is associated with Persian governors, not Akkadians, Babylonians, or Egyptians.

8. B: Of the cultures listed, only the Hebrews worshipped one God. Egyptians, Sumerians, Babylonians, and Hittites all practiced polytheistic religions that worshipped a host of deities.

9. B: Enkidu, is a character in the *Epic of Gilgamesh.* Ahura Mazda is a deity in the Zoroastrian religion. Yahweh is the God of the Hebrew people. Thoth is one of the many Egyptian deities. Zoroaster is the prophet of the Zoroastrian religion.

10. B: Abraham is considered the founder of the Israelite tradition. Zoroaster is not directly associated with the Israelite tradition. Aeneas is a character from Greek legends, sometimes associated with the founding of Rome. Though Daniel and Jesus shaped the history of the Israelite people and religion, neither is considered the founder.

11. E: Ziggurats are tall stair-stepped towers built by Mesopotamians. The remaining choices are true: The Phoenicians developed purple dyes associated with royalty, sailing technology used all over the ancient world, an alphabet which formed the foundation of many writing systems still in use, and influential metalworking practices.

12. D: Around 600 BC, the Lydians of Asia Minor were one of the first to coin metal currency.

Copyright © Mometrix Media. You have been licensed one copy of this document for personal use only. Any other reproduction or redistribution is strictly prohibited. All rights reserved.
This content is provided for test preparation purposes only and does not imply an endorsement by Mometrix of any particular political, scientific, or religious point of view.

13. C: *C* is the best choice because Athenian culture developed more than a thousand years later than Minoan. The remaining choices all reflect true statements, so none is the best choice for the question. The legendary King Minos is the namesake for the island. Knossos was the center of Minoan culture and its capital was on the island of Crete. The capital was a mazelike structure from which we derive the term "labyrinth." Many frescoes, or wall paintings, have been uncovered and reconstructed provide scholars a great source of information about Minoan culture.

14. A: The word "democracy" comes from two Greek root words: *demos* "people" and *kratia* "rule."

15. A: Members of the slave class of ancient Sparta were called helots. Hoplites, refers to a type of foot soldier. The ephorate was a governing body in Sparta. Metics is a term that refers to a class of people living in Athens who were not Athenian citizens by birth and who could not own land or run for political office. Archon refers to a governing body in Athens that assumed the duties of the former kings.

16. A: Draco was an Athenian who sentenced offenders to death for minor infractions. The word "Draconian" is still used today to refer to unusually harsh punishments. Solon is the legendary reformer of the Athenian legal system. Alcibiades is an Athenian famous for leading the navy in a disastrous campaign in Sicily. Pericles is the Athenian leader who incurred the resentment of other city-states in ancient Greece because of the amount of power he amassed. Aristophanes is considered the greatest author of comedies of the classical period.

17. C: Each of the statements is true except *C*. The historical record indicates the Greeks were outnumbered by the Persians many times over. Persian forces did invade the Greek mainland in retaliation for Athens' involvement in an uprising against Persian Satraps in Asia Minor. Greek soldiers did repel the Persian army at the battle of Marathon. Persian forces did penetrate the Greek's defenses and sack Athens. Athens and Sparta did align themselves against Persia in their defense of the Greek mainland.

18. D: The *Iliad* and *Odyssey* were most likely composed in the 8th Century, B.C., not during the golden age of Pericles, which lasted from the end of the Persian Wars in 448 B.C. to the beginning of the Peloponnesian Wars in 404 B.C. Pericles' oversight of Athens coincides directly with the life of Socrates, the great philosopher. The Acropolis was restored during Pericles' time. The art form of the tragedy flourished while Pericles was in power. The famous histories of Herodotus and Thucydides were written during Pericles' time.

19. D: Athens did not invade Sparta. Athens' power did create resentment among other Greek city-states. Athens' monopoly on trade accounts for a significant cause of the war. Sparta did establish an alliance to counteract the power of Athens. The Spartans did invade Attica, an area near Athens.

20. B: The *Odyssey* focuses on Odysseus, but he is only one of many characters depicted in the *Iliad.* Both epics deal with the Trojan War or its aftermath. Both works are attributed to Homer, even if some scholars have reason to doubt the attribution. The works appear to be written in the 8th Century, B.C. Both poems extend from an oral tradition.

21. C: Athena was the goddess of war, wisdom, and the arts. Aphrodite was the goddess of love. Hera was the goddess of marriage. Demeter was an Earth goddess, whose name comes from a combination of the words "Earth" and "mother." Artemis was often depicted as the goddess of the hunt.

22. B: The word derives from the Greek word for wisdom, which is also the root of "philosophy" and "sophisticated." Philosophers is not as accurate as sophists. Rhetoricians and orators refer to

Copyright © Mometrix Media. You have been licensed one copy of this document for personal use only. Any other reproduction or redistribution is strictly prohibited. All rights reserved.
This content is provided for test preparation purposes only and does not imply an endorsement by Mometrix of any particular political, scientific, or religious point of view.

public speakers, not private tutors. Although the sophists vetted their students for a life in politics, politicians were primarily educators.

23. C: Athenian women were not allowed to vote. The other choices are all true of Athenian women. Many families practiced infanticide, killing female infants. Women were expected to govern the household. The public domain was not considered the proper place for a woman. Women were not allowed to own or inherit any property.

24. B: Phillip of Macedon defeated Greek troops in the Battle of Chaeronea in 338 B.C. The remaining choices are incorrect.

25. E: A, B, and C are implausible or historically inaccurate. D is incorrect because Rome did not begin to expand its empire during these decades.

26. C: Each of these statements is historically true except *C*. Alexander did not successfully conquer all of India because his troops, weary from years of military campaigns, mutinied. Alexander agreed to return home and conquered many tribes along the western border of the country, but he did not enter the mainland as he intended.

27. D: Alexander's son did not bring peace to the region; he was executed after taking power over the empire. Each of the remaining choices is true statements about the period after Alexander's death.

28. B: The Greeks believed excess brought about negative consequences, while moderation did not. The remaining choices reflect other cultures' values, some of which are present in Greek culture; however, the theme of moderation dominates Greek writing and art.

29. C: The belief that humanity has fallen from grace is more in keeping with Christian beliefs. Furthermore, the faces of Greek statues rarely express humility. The expressionless faces of Greek statuary capture the belief that strong emotion should not be expressed in public. Each of the remaining statements is a valid interpretation. The symmetry and precision of Greek architecture was achieved through the application of geometrical and mathematical principles. The Greeks placed a high value on athletic skill as evidenced in the popularity of the Olympic Games. Much Greek art was functional. Simplicity was valued above excess and this value is reflected in the art.

30. B: The majority of our knowledge of Socrates' philosophy comes from the writing of Plato, and to a lesser extent, the writing of his contemporary, Xenophon. Socrates never wrote anything down. In one of Plato's dialogs, he speaks out against the written word, arguing that it makes the memory weaker if people become too reliant on it. The comedian Aristophanes did depict Socrates in his play *The Clouds,* however, the comedic work only parodies and doesn't explore in any depth. Many works about Socrates were written during his lifetime and shortly thereafter.

31. A: The most significant clue is the name Pyrrho, who founded the school of skepticism. Epicureanism held that people should seek pleasure and minimize pain to get the most out of life. The cynics promoted a life without concern for social status, physical pleasure, or wealth. The stoics placed the pursuit of wisdom above all other goals. Dualism is a generic term for a philosophy that divides the world into two parts: mind / body, spiritual / material, etc.

32. E: Democritus was a Greek philosopher whose argument that the world is composed of tiny, indivisible atoms has been confirmed by science. The atomic theory is primarily attributed to Democritus and his mentor Leucippus.

Copyright © Mometrix Media. You have been licensed one copy of this document for personal use only. Any other reproduction or redistribution is strictly prohibited. All rights reserved.
This content is provided for test preparation purposes only and does not imply an endorsement by Mometrix of any particular political, scientific, or religious point of view.

33. B: Socrates is not considered the first to argue in favor of the atomic theory. The remaining choices are true statements about the contributions of Greek thinkers to science.

34. A: The three works are the only extant trilogy, though most works of Greek drama were composed as trilogies. The three plays written about Oedipus were written by Sophocles and were not technically a trilogy. Sophocles' plays were composed and performed at different times while Aeschylus' works were composed to be performed together. The remaining choices are not trilogies.

35. A: Herodotus' *Histories* tells the story of the Persian invasion of Greece. It covers many historical topics, but its central focus is the Persian Wars. *B* is associated with the Trojan War, which is not the main subject of Herodotus' work. *C* is covered by Thucydides in *The History of the Peloponnesian Wars. D*, the legend of King Oedipus, was depicted in Sophocles' dramatic works. E: reflects the content of many plays and epics, but not the central focus of Herodotus' *Histories.*

36. E: Plato is the philosopher described in the passage. Aristotle famously disagreed with the theory of forms, preferring to focus on the natural world itself instead of the ideal world of forms that Plato described. Thales is primarily remembered for his contributions to geometry and his belief that water is the principle element from which all matter extends. Anaxagoras is best remembered for his mathematical arguments and his theory that material substances are the result of an immaterial force or spirit that he called "nous," which translates as "mind." Parmenides is remembered for his use of logical deduction to determine the fundamental principles of nature.

37. B: The harsh educational techniques were practiced in Sparta, not Athens. The remaining choices are all reflections of Athenian educational practice.

38. B: The Etruscans were from a kingdom to the north that seized control of Rome from the Latins in the mid-600s BC. They began urbanizing the settlement, improving roads, adding drainage systems, etc. They were driven out of the region in 509 BC during an uprising of the Latins.

39. C: The city of Rome was founded around 753 B.C. The remaining statements are true of the Latins.

40. A: This passage describes the Senate. The Magistrates were composed of several groups, each with different responsibilities. The remaining choices were all part of the Magistrates. Praetors were responsible for overseeing the legal system and the army. The Censors enforced the moral code of the Romans. The Consuls were two chief executives who made important decisions for the Republic. Their ability to veto one another is one of the earliest examples of a system of checks and balances.

41. D: The effects of the Punic Wars include the development of a strong Roman naval force, the destruction of Carthage, the increased influence of Rome in the region, and the loss of Macedonian influence.

42. D: The Conflict of the Orders refers to a disagreement between Roman commoners, the Plebeians and the wealthy aristocracy, the Patricians. Until the 4th Century B.C., Patricians had complete control of the Roman Senate and held great political power in spite of representing only a small percentage of the population. The Patricians routinely abused their power, for example, selling wealthy Plebeians into slavery if they failed to repay debts. Plebeians, wealthy landowners in particular, undertook a variety of largely peaceful protests and were awarded political representation in 287 B.C. These events led to the composition of the "Twelve Tables," legal documents, which became the foundation of Roman law.

Copyright © Mometrix Media. You have been licensed one copy of this document for personal use only. Any other reproduction or redistribution is strictly prohibited. All rights reserved.
This content is provided for test preparation purposes only and does not imply an endorsement by Mometrix of any particular political, scientific, or religious point of view.

43. C: The remaining events occurred throughout the Punic Wars, but none identifies the primary event that sparked the wars. *A* triggered the Second Punic War in 218 B.C. *B* took place in 146 B.C. at the end of the Punic Wars. *D* happened after the Second Punic War in 197 B.C. *E* occurred in 204 B.C., during the Second Punic War.

44. B: Caesar's political rivals and former allies assassinated him because they feared his power. *A* is true of Tiberius. *C* describes an infamous political appointment made by Caligula. *D* recounts one of Caesar's famous military actions, but was not the principle reason for his assassination. *E* is true of Marc Antony, who attacked Augustus in 31 B.C., after Caesar's death.

45. E: Marcus Aurelius, is the only emperor among those listed who was not a member of the Julio-Claudian line. The first emperor from this family lineage was Augustus. He was followed by Tiberius, Caligula and Claudius. The lineage ended in 68 A.D. with the suicide of Nero.

46. A: *B* refers to several influential tribunes and consuls from the 1st and 2nd Centuries B.C. C: is the three emperors who took power and were assassinated in the year following Nero's suicide. *D* refers to the five claimants to the throne in the year 193 A.D. *E* is the five emperors from the Julio-Claudian line.

47. C: The passage describes the 200-year period known as *Pax Romana. A* is incorrect because the Julio-Claudian line held power in Rome for less than a century. *B* refers to a succession of emperors that lasted less than one hundred years. The emperors in *D* only ruled from 69 A.D. to 96 A.D. *E* is two tribunes who attempted to lead reforms in the 2nd Century B.C.

48. C: The Forum, the Pantheon, the Coliseum and the House of the Vestal Virgins are all major structures in the city of Rome. Hadrian's Wall is in England.

49. C: Spartacus was the leader of a slave rebellion.

50. D: Homer is the ancient Greek author of the *Iliad* and the *Odyssey*. Horace was a Roman poet, the source of many popular Latin phrases, such as *carpe diem*, "seize the day." His works include *Odes*, *Satires*, and *Ars Poetica.* Livy was a famous Roman historian whose only surviving work is the *History of Rome*. Plutarch wrote many works. One of his best known works is a collection of biographies, referred to as *Lives*, which recount the lives of great Greek figures and compare them to great Romans. Each contains a philosophical reflection on the lessons to be learned from each figure's accomplishments and character. Virgil is best known for his epic, the *Aeneid*, which recounts the mythical history of Rome and connects the country's origins to the great Greeks who fought in the Trojan War.

51. C: The *Metamorphoses* collects many Roman and Greek myths. The book was written in 8 A.D. and was the primary source for understanding Greek mythology throughout the medieval period. Ovid had a huge impact on Shakespeare.

52. C: Starting with Edward Gibbon's tome, *The Decline and Fall of the Roman Empire*, many historians attributed the gradual decline of power in Rome to moral corruption. These historians often cite the bloody gladiator battles and executions as examples of the deterioration of Roman morals.

53. B: Paul of Tarsus played one of the most significant roles in the development of the early Christian Church.

Copyright © Mometrix Media. You have been licensed one copy of this document for personal use only. Any other reproduction or redistribution is strictly prohibited. All rights reserved.
This content is provided for test preparation purposes only and does not imply an endorsement by Mometrix of any particular political, scientific, or religious point of view.

54. A: As part of a larger effort to combat supporters of pagan religions in Rome, Theodosius made Christianity the official religion of the Roman Empire in 391 A.D.

55. E: The Etruscans invaded Rome much earlier in its history and had no part in the Germanic invasions of the 5th through 7th Centuries A.D. The Goths, the Ostrogoths and the Visigoths sacked Rome in 410 A.D. The Vandals were the second group to plunder Rome in 455 A.D. The term "vandalism" comes from the destruction this group caused and from their unrestrained looting of Rome's wealth and art. The Huns attacked many Roman territories in the middle of the 5th Century.

56. C: It is the only one that does NOT contribute to the split between the eastern and western Empires. The Crusades did not begin until the 11th Century A.D. Emperor Diocletian attempted to make the empire easier to rule by dividing it into two separate centers of control, which established a precedent for separating the eastern empire from the western. Though emperors after Diocletian did succeed in reuniting the empire, corruption threatened to tear the kingdom apart again. Over time, Constantinople, the seat of power in the eastern Empire, amassed more power and influence. The gap between the rich and poor widened considerably in the West, leading to a loss of faith in the government and a gradual decline in strength. Constantinople and the eastern empire continued to thrive.

57. A: Most of the conquered peoples were not granted Roman citizenship. Each conquered state was allowed some degree of cultural autonomy. Subjects were expected to follow the laws of Rome, pay taxes, and hand over land and supplies to the Roman government.

58. A: The Justinian Code was a collection of Roman laws and legal opinions. In the 6th Century A.D., Justinian assembled a collection of jurists to bring together the most important works of Roman law including public laws and legal opinions.

59. B: The iconoclasts opposed *B*, the use of religious images, or icons, in worship. *E* does reflect part of the argument made by proponents of icons, namely that it helped to spread Christianity to the illiterate masses. By the 7th Century A.D., images of Jesus and the saints gained popularity for use in worship. Many Christians believed that the worship of images was a false form of religion. In the 8th Century, Emperor Leo III of Byzantium and Pope Adrian I outlawed the worship of icons. This decision eventually led to the split between the Roman Catholic and Eastern Orthodox Churches.

60. E: The first obligation of Islam, the profession of faith, is "shahadah." The second requirement, five daily prayers, is "salat." Contributing to the poor and needy is the third obligation, "zakat." A pilgrimage to the city of Mecca "hajj," is the fifth requirement. Not listed is the fourth pillar, "sawm," fasting during the day for one month of the year.

61. B: Imam refers to leaders of the Shiite sect. Sultan refers to a Turkish Muslim government leader. Sheik refers to an elder or leader in an Arabic tribe. Vizier was a member of the Turkish Islamic government.

62. D: Each answer describes a significant contribution Arabic thinkers made to the sciences except D, the abacus, which predates Arabic culture.

63. D: Each answers presents one of the main reasons Europe entered a period of fragmentation, referred to as the "Dark Ages," except D. There was no global collapse of civilization during this time; sciences and arts continued to flourish in many other cultures.

Copyright © Mometrix Media. You have been licensed one copy of this document for personal use only. Any other reproduction or redistribution is strictly prohibited. All rights reserved.
This content is provided for test preparation purposes only and does not imply an endorsement by Mometrix of any particular political, scientific, or religious point of view.

64. A: The person described in this passage is Charlemagne, King of the Franks (742-814). Pope Leo III was a contemporary and ally of Charlemagne. Charles Martel was best known for halting Muslim expansion by defeating invading armies at the Battle of Tours in 732. Clovis I and Pepin II were both responsible for bringing unity to the Frankish tribes.

65. C: Fief refers to the section of land a lord might grant. Homage refers to the oath of loyalty the recipient of the land would make to the lord. Primogeniture refers to the system of inheritance that granted the son of a lord complete ownership and control of his landholdings. Vassal is the person who would receive land from the lord.

66. C: Each statement accurately describes the system of manorialism except *C*. Serfs could not, as a rule, become nobles by working hard.

67. D: Each statement describes the hierarchy of the Catholic Church except *D*. The curia was a group of archbishops who elected new popes, but the ultimate authority was the pope.

68. B: Heretic is a term used to describe one who has been excommunicated. Interdict refers to the church's authority to keep entire regions from receiving the sacraments. Canon law refers to the code of law that governed the church. Indulgences refer to the widely criticized practice of charging fees for the forgiveness of sins.

69. E: The practice of chivalry refers to a code of conduct among knights. Serfs were peasants who worked the land and gave the crops to the lord, keeping enough for their own sustenance. Archbishops were members of the Roman Catholic church hierarchy. Troubadours were travelling musicians whose songs about chivalry kept the code alive in the popular imagination. Vassals were nobles who received land from lords in compensation for their loyalty and protection.

70. A: *B* refers to Geoffrey Chaucer. *C* refers to Dante Alighieri. *D* refers to St. Francis of Assisi. *E* refers to the work of St. Augustine.

71. D: Charters refer to land grants that allowed citizens of towns certain rights. Fief refers to a land granted by a lord to a vassal, a lower noble, in exchange for loyalty and protection. Manor refers to a lord's landholdings. Banks refers to moneychangers.

72. B: The Black Death refers to the plague that swept through 14th century Europe. Bubonic plague, brought in by rats on shipping vessels, is believed to have been the primary cause, though some question this theory.

73. E: The Angles and Saxons were two of the Germanic groups who competed for power after the fall of Rome. It is from them that the term Anglo-Saxons originated.

74. D: Each of the answers describes a key event of the year 1066 except *D*. The English army did not avoid battle. The Battle of Hastings was a bloody conflict that resulted in the devastation of the English army. William the Conqueror took control of England and brought Norman customs and government, which shaped the culture of England.

75. B: Each of the answers is true except *B*. The Magna Carta did not take the powers of the monarchy away. It did, however, hold the monarchy to the same rule of law as commoners.

76. A: Joan of Arc was a French peasant who had visions of saints telling her to lead the French army in an attack against the English. She eventually led the French to a victorious battle against

Copyright © Mometrix Media. You have been licensed one copy of this document for personal use only. Any other reproduction or redistribution is strictly prohibited. All rights reserved.
This content is provided for test preparation purposes only and does not imply an endorsement by Mometrix of any particular political, scientific, or religious point of view.

the English in 1429. Several years later she was brought before the Inquisition by political enemies, found guilty of heresy, and sentenced to death.

77. E: Each of the choices is true except *E*. The Crusades occurred before the Inquisition.

78. A: None of the other answers applies to the Inquisition. These historical events began in 1224 when Pope Gregory IX began investigating, torturing and executing suspected heretics. These measures were initially undertaken to combat the growing threat of Christian sects that sought to undermine the authority of the Catholic Church.

79. C: Each of the answers is true of the Great Schism except *C*. The Catholic Church split into eastern and western factions in 1054. The Great Schism refers to the splintering of the Catholic Church's power as the kings of several different regions attempted to install their own popes.

80. C: John Wycliffe and Jan Hus were early reformers of the Catholic Church who believed that individuals should be educated and that bishops and clergy held too much power. Pope Leo III was in power during the reign of Charlemagne. Martin Luther was a church reformer who eventually split with the Catholic Church, sparking the Protestant Reformation.

81. C: The Reformation refers to a time when attempts to reform the Catholic Church led to a split between Catholic and Protestant groups. The Middle Ages refers to the period between the fall of the Roman Empire and the beginning of the Renaissance, an era sometimes referred to as the "Dark Ages." The Counter Reformation was a period when the pope attempted to address the criticisms of Protestant reformers and reform the Catholic Church. The Scientific Revolution refers to a period when traditional interpretations of the natural world were replaced with interpretations based on the scientific method of careful observation.

82. A: The Medici were a powerful, wealthy family, famous for their financial contributions to artists in Florence.

83. E: Brunelleschi was an architect whose most famous construction is the Duomo in Florence. Masaccio was a painter whose frescoes demonstrate an early attempt to develop perspective that would later give Renaissance paintings their striking realism. Lorenzo Ghiberti was a sculptor noted for his "Gates of Paradise," the doors of the cathedral in Florence, adorned with sculptures depicting biblical scenes. Botticelli was a noted painter whose works include *Primavera* and *Birth of Venus.*

84. A: Scholasticism refers to the work of St. Thomas Aquinas who attempted to use formal logic to address issues of divinity and Christian faith. Philosophy is a very broad term encompassing humanism and many other intellectual movements. Syncretism refers to the practice of reconciling contradictory beliefs between religions. Classicism refers to students of Ancient Greek and Roman culture. Though the humanists were students of the classics, their work reflects a philosophy different from strict classicism.

85. E: The *Mona Lisa,* is the only painting not created by Michelangelo. The artist was Leonardo Da Vinci.

86. B: Though choices *C*, *D*, and *E* apply to Da Vinci, the question describes him as a man with great learning and skills in a variety of fields, which is the definition of a Renaissance Man.

87. E: Raphael, is the only artist not a member of the Flemish school. Jan and Hubert van Eyck were brothers who perfected of the technique of oil painting. Brueghel often depicted images of peasants

Copyright © Mometrix Media. You have been licensed one copy of this document for personal use only. Any other reproduction or redistribution is strictly prohibited. All rights reserved.
This content is provided for test preparation purposes only and does not imply an endorsement by Mometrix of any particular political, scientific, or religious point of view.

in order to criticize the injustices he witnessed. Gerard David was renowned for the use of colors in his illustrated manuscripts and miniatures.

88. D: Thomas More, was the author of *Utopia* that described an ideal society with no private property and equality for all.

89. A: Ivan the Terrible, also known as Ivan IV, is the Russian king described. Michael Romanov would come to power in Russia after Ivan's reign. Genghis Khan conquered Russia in the 13th Century before Ivan's reign. Ivan the Terrible was a member of the Rurik lineage, which included his father, Ivan the Great, and the first of the Ivans to rule Russia, Ivan I.

90. D: Kiev, is part of Russia. The other choices were separate Kingdoms in the Iberian Peninsula — the area known as Spain — until Ferdinand and Isabella began consolidating the regions in the late 15th Century.

91. C: A devout Catholic, Mary Tudor was known as "Bloody Mary" for her violent opposition to members of the Anglican Church, which her father, Henry VIII, created. She once burned 300 religious dissidents at the stake.

92. A: The term "indulgence" refers to the Catholic practice of priests reducing the punishment for a sin. In the 16th Century when priests began charging a fee for indulgences, Martin Luther vehemently opposed abuses related to indulgences.

93. C: Each shows a significant consequence of the printing press except *C*. The Great Schism took place in the 14th and 15th Centuries when kings and other political influences began to erode the authority of the Catholic Church.

94. B: Each of the other statements reflects one of Martin Luther's core beliefs.

95. B: Accounts for Henry VIII's decision to create the Anglican Church. He wanted a male heir, but his marriage to Catherine of Aragon gave him only daughters. When he requested a divorce, Pope Clement VII denied him. In response, he joined the Protestant movement and established the Anglican Church.

96. A: The queen described is Elizabeth I. Anne Boleyn was Henry VIII's second wife, stepmother to Elizabeth I. Mary Tudor was Elizabeth's sister, known as "Bloody Mary." Catherine of Aragon was Henry VIII's first wife, Elizabeth's mother. Isabella was the Queen of Spain.

97. C: The doctrine of the Eucharist. Martin Luther believed that Christ was physically present "in, around, and under" the elements, while John Calvin believed that Christ was not physically present (yet still spiritually present) in the Eucharist. Neither opposed the remaining choices: Jesus's divinity, the Trinity, the need for reform in the Catholic Church, or the doctrine of justification by faith alone.

98. D: The Counter Reformation was a 16th Century movement that wanted to reform the Catholic Church without losing its traditions. It began roughly with the Council of Trent (1545-1643) and ended with the Thirty Years War (1648).

99. D: The Council of Trent met to determine what aspects of Protestant doctrine it considered heretical and to define the Church's position on key issues of the Catholic faith.

100. E: Machiavelli's book *The Prince* promoted a shrewd approach to politics, aimed at maintaining power. Petrarch was a humanist poet, famous for his sonnets. Castiglione wrote a

Copyright © Mometrix Media. You have been licensed one copy of this document for personal use only. Any other reproduction or redistribution is strictly prohibited. All rights reserved.
This content is provided for test preparation purposes only and does not imply an endorsement by Mometrix of any particular political, scientific, or religious point of view.

novel disguised as fiction that revealed the lives of government officials and royalty. Brunelleschi was an architect famous for the Duomo. Botticelli was an influential painter from Florence, Italy.

101. B: Moscow took the nickname the "Third Rome," after the fall of Constantinople because it became the center of the Orthodox Church. Since Rome was the first center of the Catholic Church and Constantinople was the second, Moscow attempted to align itself with these great cities.

102. E: Ignatius Loyola founded an order of priests called the Society of Jesus, or Jesuits. Amerigo Vespucci was immortalized when German mapmakers named the new world after him. Magellan was a Portuguese explorer who led the first expedition to travel around the world. John Cabot claimed Newfoundland, Nova Scotia, and areas of New England for England. Henry Hudson explored much of what is now the northeastern United States.

103. B: The witch hunts reflect a time when belief in magic and superstition was widespread. Many historians view them as a reaction to the social and economic changes of the Early Modern period.

104. E: The steam engine was not invented until the 19th Century. The other choices describe a technological innovation that helped improve navigation and shipbuilding technology during the Early Modern period.

105. B: While much drought, famine, and war took place in Europe, none of these events completely destroyed the region. Many people remained in Europe despite expansion abroad.

106. D: Triangular trade refers to the process by which Europeans exchanged goods and slaves with the Americas.

107. B: The Dutch East India Company named the region after the city of Amsterdam. The city was renamed after the British took control of the region in 1664.

108. B: Members of Spanish and British royalty conspired to assassinate Elizabeth I, Queen of England. *C* refers to attacks against the region of Spain in the 700s. *D* is an incorrect statement: England financed the seadogs, pirates who attacked Spanish vessels. *E* is an incorrect statement: the uprising in the Netherlands was against Spain.

109. A: The Thirty Years' War began when the Holy Roman Emperor began to drive Protestants from Bohemia and Austria in 1618. Protestants responded by rebelling, and though they were quickly suppressed, many other rebellions began. They sparked a land-grab in the region, which was finally settled in 1648 with the Treaty of Westphalia, creating several new nations in Eastern Europe.

110. B: The Long Parliament refers to the reign of Charles I whose attempts to raise taxes were repeatedly thwarted by Parliament. In response, Charles refused to allow Parliament to convene for eleven years and attempted to rule England as an absolute monarchy. In 1640, when Charles convened Parliament to help settle a Scottish uprising, Parliament passed laws limiting his power to convene and disband Parliament.

111. B: Though Elizabeth publicly disavowed the group of pirates known as the seadogs, claiming she had no influence or control over their actions, she privately funded their raids on rival countries' sea vessels.

112. D: The Moors invaded Spain in the 700s. Although Spain's decline in power began to accelerate after the defeat of the Spanish Armada, many causes led up to the decline.

Copyright © Mometrix Media. You have been licensed one copy of this document for personal use only. Any other reproduction or redistribution is strictly prohibited. All rights reserved.
This content is provided for test preparation purposes only and does not imply an endorsement by Mometrix of any particular political, scientific, or religious point of view.

113. A: After the period known as the Long Parliament when King Charles I refused to convene Parliament, members of the government attempted to take control of the army. In response, Charles had several leaders of the House of Commons arrested. Soon after, fighting broke out between factions loyal to Charles, known as the Cavaliers, and supporters of Parliament, called the Roundheads.

114. B: The Scientific Revolution emphasized careful observation of the natural world and applied reason to make and test generalizations about how it operated. The Scientific Revolution saw its zenith in the wide-ranging discoveries of Sir Isaac Newton (1642-1727).

115. B: The *Dialogue Concerning the Two Chief World Systems* was written in 1632 by Galileo Galilei. Two characters debate the merits and flaws of the Ptolemaic model, the Earth was the center of the heavens, and the Copernican model, the Earth was not the center of the universe. The Inquisition forced Galileo to publicly retract his support for the Copernican model.

116. C: Francis Bacon was an English philosopher who promoted the scientific method. Roger Bacon was a monk who argued in favor of scientific experimentation to better understand the physical world. Ambroise Paré is considered the father of modern surgery. Andreas Vesalius made an important impact on the study of anatomy.

117. A: The Puritans believed the Anglican Church needed to be purified (hence the name "Puritans": of all remnants of Catholicism.

118. B: The town described is *B*, Jamestown. Plymouth was founded by Puritan settlers in pursuit of religious freedom. Charleston was also known for its religious tolerance. St. Augustine was founded in 1565 by Spanish settlers and is the oldest continuously inhabited city in the US Salem was an important seaport.

119. D: Despite the growing amount of literacy in the 1500s, due principally to the invention of the printing press and the availability of texts, the majority of Europeans remained illiterate.

120. B: Preservatives such as salt were only introduced to the European diet after trade routes opened and these goods could be brought to Europe.

Copyright © Mometrix Media. You have been licensed one copy of this document for personal use only. Any other reproduction or redistribution is strictly prohibited. All rights reserved.
This content is provided for test preparation purposes only and does not imply an endorsement by Mometrix of any particular political, scientific, or religious point of view.

How to Overcome Test Anxiety

Just the thought of taking a test is enough to make most people a little nervous. A test is an important event that can have a long-term impact on your future, so it's important to take it seriously and it's natural to feel anxious about performing well. But just because anxiety is normal, that doesn't mean that it's helpful in test taking, or that you should simply accept it as part of your life. Anxiety can have a variety of effects. These effects can be mild, like making you feel slightly nervous, or severe, like blocking your ability to focus or remember even a simple detail.

If you experience test anxiety—whether severe or mild—it's important to know how to beat it. To discover this, first you need to understand what causes test anxiety.

Causes of Test Anxiety

While we often think of anxiety as an uncontrollable emotional state, it can actually be caused by simple, practical things. One of the most common causes of test anxiety is that a person does not feel adequately prepared for their test. This feeling can be the result of many different issues such as poor study habits or lack of organization, but the most common culprit is time management. Starting to study too late, failing to organize your study time to cover all of the material, or being distracted while you study will mean that you're not well prepared for the test. This may lead to cramming the night before, which will cause you to be physically and mentally exhausted for the test. Poor time management also contributes to feelings of stress, fear, and hopelessness as you realize you are not well prepared but don't know what to do about it.

Other times, test anxiety is not related to your preparation for the test but comes from unresolved fear. This may be a past failure on a test, or poor performance on tests in general. It may come from comparing yourself to others who seem to be performing better or from the stress of living up to expectations. Anxiety may be driven by fears of the future—how failure on this test would affect your educational and career goals. These fears are often completely irrational, but they can still negatively impact your test performance.

Elements of Test Anxiety

As mentioned earlier, test anxiety is considered to be an emotional state, but it has physical and mental components as well. Sometimes you may not even realize that you are suffering from test anxiety until you notice the physical symptoms. These can include trembling hands, rapid heartbeat, sweating, nausea, and tense muscles. Extreme anxiety may lead to fainting or vomiting. Obviously, any of these symptoms can have a negative impact on testing. It is important to recognize them as soon as they begin to occur so that you can address the problem before it damages your performance.

The mental components of test anxiety include trouble focusing and inability to remember learned information. During a test, your mind is on high alert, which can help you recall information and stay focused for an extended period of time. However, anxiety interferes with your mind's natural processes, causing you to blank out, even on the questions you know well. The strain of testing during anxiety makes it difficult to stay focused, especially on a test that may take several hours. Extreme anxiety can take a huge mental toll, making it difficult not only to recall test information but even to understand the test questions or pull your thoughts together.

Copyright © Mometrix Media. You have been licensed one copy of this document for personal use only. Any other reproduction or redistribution is strictly prohibited. All rights reserved.
This content is provided for test preparation purposes only and does not imply an endorsement by Mometrix of any particular political, scientific, or religious point of view.

Effects of Test Anxiety

Test anxiety is like a disease—if left untreated, it will get progressively worse. Anxiety leads to poor performance, and this reinforces the feelings of fear and failure, which in turn lead to poor performances on subsequent tests. It can grow from a mild nervousness to a crippling condition. If allowed to progress, test anxiety can have a big impact on your schooling, and consequently on your future.

Test anxiety can spread to other parts of your life. Anxiety on tests can become anxiety in any stressful situation, and blanking on a test can turn into panicking in a job situation. But fortunately, you don't have to let anxiety rule your testing and determine your grades. There are a number of relatively simple steps you can take to move past anxiety and function normally on a test and in the rest of life.

Physical Steps for Beating Test Anxiety

While test anxiety is a serious problem, the good news is that it can be overcome. It doesn't have to control your ability to think and remember information. While it may take time, you can begin taking steps today to beat anxiety.

Just as your first hint that you may be struggling with anxiety comes from the physical symptoms, the first step to treating it is also physical. Rest is crucial for having a clear, strong mind. If you are tired, it is much easier to give in to anxiety. But if you establish good sleep habits, your body and mind will be ready to perform optimally, without the strain of exhaustion. Additionally, sleeping well helps you to retain information better, so you're more likely to recall the answers when you see the test questions.

Getting good sleep means more than going to bed on time. It's important to allow your brain time to relax. Take study breaks from time to time so it doesn't get overworked, and don't study right before bed. Take time to rest your mind before trying to rest your body, or you may find it difficult to fall asleep.

Along with sleep, other aspects of physical health are important in preparing for a test. Good nutrition is vital for good brain function. Sugary foods and drinks may give a burst of energy but this burst is followed by a crash, both physically and emotionally. Instead, fuel your body with protein and vitamin-rich foods.

Also, drink plenty of water. Dehydration can lead to headaches and exhaustion, especially if your brain is already under stress from the rigors of the test. Particularly if your test is a long one, drink water during the breaks. And if possible, take an energy-boosting snack to eat between sections.

Along with sleep and diet, a third important part of physical health is exercise. Maintaining a steady workout schedule is helpful, but even taking 5-minute study breaks to walk can help get your blood pumping faster and clear your head. Exercise also releases endorphins, which contribute to a positive feeling and can help combat test anxiety.

When you nurture your physical health, you are also contributing to your mental health. If your body is healthy, your mind is much more likely to be healthy as well. So take time to rest, nourish your body with healthy food and water, and get moving as much as possible. Taking these physical steps will make you stronger and more able to take the mental steps necessary to overcome test anxiety.

Copyright © Mometrix Media. You have been licensed one copy of this document for personal use only. Any other reproduction or redistribution is strictly prohibited. All rights reserved.
This content is provided for test preparation purposes only and does not imply an endorsement by Mometrix of any particular political, scientific, or religious point of view.

Mental Steps for Beating Test Anxiety

Working on the mental side of test anxiety can be more challenging, but as with the physical side, there are clear steps you can take to overcome it. As mentioned earlier, test anxiety often stems from lack of preparation, so the obvious solution is to prepare for the test. Effective studying may be the most important weapon you have for beating test anxiety, but you can and should employ several other mental tools to combat fear.

First, boost your confidence by reminding yourself of past success—tests or projects that you aced. If you're putting as much effort into preparing for this test as you did for those, there's no reason you should expect to fail here. Work hard to prepare; then trust your preparation.

Second, surround yourself with encouraging people. It can be helpful to find a study group, but be sure that the people you're around will encourage a positive attitude. If you spend time with others who are anxious or cynical, this will only contribute to your own anxiety. Look for others who are motivated to study hard from a desire to succeed, not from a fear of failure.

Third, reward yourself. A test is physically and mentally tiring, even without anxiety, and it can be helpful to have something to look forward to. Plan an activity following the test, regardless of the outcome, such as going to a movie or getting ice cream.

When you are taking the test, if you find yourself beginning to feel anxious, remind yourself that you know the material. Visualize successfully completing the test. Then take a few deep, relaxing breaths and return to it. Work through the questions carefully but with confidence, knowing that you are capable of succeeding.

Developing a healthy mental approach to test taking will also aid in other areas of life. Test anxiety affects more than just the actual test—it can be damaging to your mental health and even contribute to depression. It's important to beat test anxiety before it becomes a problem for more than testing.

Study Strategy

Being prepared for the test is necessary to combat anxiety, but what does being prepared look like? You may study for hours on end and still not feel prepared. What you need is a strategy for test prep. The next few pages outline our recommended steps to help you plan out and conquer the challenge of preparation.

Step 1: Scope Out the Test

Learn everything you can about the format (multiple choice, essay, etc.) and what will be on the test. Gather any study materials, course outlines, or sample exams that may be available. Not only will this help you to prepare, but knowing what to expect can help to alleviate test anxiety.

Step 2: Map Out the Material

Look through the textbook or study guide and make note of how many chapters or sections it has. Then divide these over the time you have. For example, if a book has 15 chapters and you have five days to study, you need to cover three chapters each day. Even better, if you have the time, leave an extra day at the end for overall review after you have gone through the material in depth.

If time is limited, you may need to prioritize the material. Look through it and make note of which sections you think you already have a good grasp on, and which need review. While you are studying, skim quickly through the familiar sections and take more time on the challenging parts.

Copyright © Mometrix Media. You have been licensed one copy of this document for personal use only. Any other reproduction or redistribution is strictly prohibited. All rights reserved.
This content is provided for test preparation purposes only and does not imply an endorsement by Mometrix of any particular political, scientific, or religious point of view.

Write out your plan so you don't get lost as you go. Having a written plan also helps you feel more in control of the study, so anxiety is less likely to arise from feeling overwhelmed at the amount to cover.

Step 3: Gather Your Tools

Decide what study method works best for you. Do you prefer to highlight in the book as you study and then go back over the highlighted portions? Or do you type out notes of the important information? Or is it helpful to make flashcards that you can carry with you? Assemble the pens, index cards, highlighters, post-it notes, and any other materials you may need so you won't be distracted by getting up to find things while you study.

If you're having a hard time retaining the information or organizing your notes, experiment with different methods. For example, try color-coding by subject with colored pens, highlighters, or post-it notes. If you learn better by hearing, try recording yourself reading your notes so you can listen while in the car, working out, or simply sitting at your desk. Ask a friend to quiz you from your flashcards, or try teaching someone the material to solidify it in your mind.

Step 4: Create Your Environment

It's important to avoid distractions while you study. This includes both the obvious distractions like visitors and the subtle distractions like an uncomfortable chair (or a too-comfortable couch that makes you want to fall asleep). Set up the best study environment possible: good lighting and a comfortable work area. If background music helps you focus, you may want to turn it on, but otherwise keep the room quiet. If you are using a computer to take notes, be sure you don't have any other windows open, especially applications like social media, games, or anything else that could distract you. Silence your phone and turn off notifications. Be sure to keep water close by so you stay hydrated while you study (but avoid unhealthy drinks and snacks).

Also, take into account the best time of day to study. Are you freshest first thing in the morning? Try to set aside some time then to work through the material. Is your mind clearer in the afternoon or evening? Schedule your study session then. Another method is to study at the same time of day that you will take the test, so that your brain gets used to working on the material at that time and will be ready to focus at test time.

Step 5: Study!

Once you have done all the study preparation, it's time to settle into the actual studying. Sit down, take a few moments to settle your mind so you can focus, and begin to follow your study plan. Don't give in to distractions or let yourself procrastinate. This is your time to prepare so you'll be ready to fearlessly approach the test. Make the most of the time and stay focused.

Of course, you don't want to burn out. If you study too long you may find that you're not retaining the information very well. Take regular study breaks. For example, taking five minutes out of every hour to walk briskly, breathing deeply and swinging your arms, can help your mind stay fresh.

As you get to the end of each chapter or section, it's a good idea to do a quick review. Remind yourself of what you learned and work on any difficult parts. When you feel that you've mastered the material, move on to the next part. At the end of your study session, briefly skim through your notes again.

But while review is helpful, cramming last minute is NOT. If at all possible, work ahead so that you won't need to fit all your study into the last day. Cramming overloads your brain with more information than it can process and retain, and your tired mind may struggle to recall even

Copyright © Mometrix Media. You have been licensed one copy of this document for personal use only. Any other reproduction or redistribution is strictly prohibited. All rights reserved.
This content is provided for test preparation purposes only and does not imply an endorsement by Mometrix of any particular political, scientific, or religious point of view.

previously learned information when it is overwhelmed with last-minute study. Also, the urgent nature of cramming and the stress placed on your brain contribute to anxiety. You'll be more likely to go to the test feeling unprepared and having trouble thinking clearly.

So don't cram, and don't stay up late before the test, even just to review your notes at a leisurely pace. Your brain needs rest more than it needs to go over the information again. In fact, plan to finish your studies by noon or early afternoon the day before the test. Give your brain the rest of the day to relax or focus on other things, and get a good night's sleep. Then you will be fresh for the test and better able to recall what you've studied.

Step 6: Take a Practice Test

Many courses offer sample tests, either online or in the study materials. This is an excellent resource to check whether you have mastered the material, as well as to prepare for the test format and environment.

Check the test format ahead of time: the number of questions, the type (multiple choice, free response, etc.), and the time limit. Then create a plan for working through them. For example, if you have 30 minutes to take a 60-question test, your limit is 30 seconds per question. Spend less time on the questions you know well so that you can take more time on the difficult ones.

If you have time to take several practice tests, take the first one open book, with no time limit. Work through the questions at your own pace and make sure you fully understand them. Gradually work up to taking a test under test conditions: sit at a desk with all study materials put away and set a timer. Pace yourself to make sure you finish the test with time to spare and go back to check your answers if you have time.

After each test, check your answers. On the questions you missed, be sure you understand why you missed them. Did you misread the question (tests can use tricky wording)? Did you forget the information? Or was it something you hadn't learned? Go back and study any shaky areas that the practice tests reveal.

Taking these tests not only helps with your grade, but also aids in combating test anxiety. If you're already used to the test conditions, you're less likely to worry about it, and working through tests until you're scoring well gives you a confidence boost. Go through the practice tests until you feel comfortable, and then you can go into the test knowing that you're ready for it.

Test Tips

On test day, you should be confident, knowing that you've prepared well and are ready to answer the questions. But aside from preparation, there are several test day strategies you can employ to maximize your performance.

First, as stated before, get a good night's sleep the night before the test (and for several nights before that, if possible). Go into the test with a fresh, alert mind rather than staying up late to study.

Try not to change too much about your normal routine on the day of the test. It's important to eat a nutritious breakfast, but if you normally don't eat breakfast at all, consider eating just a protein bar. If you're a coffee drinker, go ahead and have your normal coffee. Just make sure you time it so that the caffeine doesn't wear off right in the middle of your test. Avoid sugary beverages, and drink enough water to stay hydrated but not so much that you need a restroom break 10 minutes into the

Copyright © Mometrix Media. You have been licensed one copy of this document for personal use only. Any other reproduction or redistribution is strictly prohibited. All rights reserved.
This content is provided for test preparation purposes only and does not imply an endorsement by Mometrix of any particular political, scientific, or religious point of view.

test. If your test isn't first thing in the morning, consider going for a walk or doing a light workout before the test to get your blood flowing.

Allow yourself enough time to get ready, and leave for the test with plenty of time to spare so you won't have the anxiety of scrambling to arrive in time. Another reason to be early is to select a good seat. It's helpful to sit away from doors and windows, which can be distracting. Find a good seat, get out your supplies, and settle your mind before the test begins.

When the test begins, start by going over the instructions carefully, even if you already know what to expect. Make sure you avoid any careless mistakes by following the directions.

Then begin working through the questions, pacing yourself as you've practiced. If you're not sure on an answer, don't spend too much time on it, and don't let it shake your confidence. Either skip it and come back later, or eliminate as many wrong answers as possible and guess among the remaining ones. Don't dwell on these questions as you continue—put them out of your mind and focus on what lies ahead.

Be sure to read all of the answer choices, even if you're sure the first one is the right answer. Sometimes you'll find a better one if you keep reading. But don't second-guess yourself if you do immediately know the answer. Your gut instinct is usually right. Don't let test anxiety rob you of the information you know.

If you have time at the end of the test (and if the test format allows), go back and review your answers. Be cautious about changing any, since your first instinct tends to be correct, but make sure you didn't misread any of the questions or accidentally mark the wrong answer choice. Look over any you skipped and make an educated guess.

At the end, leave the test feeling confident. You've done your best, so don't waste time worrying about your performance or wishing you could change anything. Instead, celebrate the successful completion of this test. And finally, use this test to learn how to deal with anxiety even better next time.

Review Video: Test Anxiety
Visit mometrix.com/academy and enter code: 100340

Important Qualification

Not all anxiety is created equal. If your test anxiety is causing major issues in your life beyond the classroom or testing center, or if you are experiencing troubling physical symptoms related to your anxiety, it may be a sign of a serious physiological or psychological condition. If this sounds like your situation, we strongly encourage you to seek professional help.

Copyright © Mometrix Media. You have been licensed one copy of this document for personal use only. Any other reproduction or redistribution is strictly prohibited. All rights reserved.
This content is provided for test preparation purposes only and does not imply an endorsement by Mometrix of any particular political, scientific, or religious point of view.

Online Resources

Due to our efforts to try to keep this book to a manageable length, we've created a link that will give you access to all of your online resources:

mometrix.com/resources719/clepwescivi

It's Your Moment, Let's Celebrate It!

Share your story @mometrixtestpreparation

Copyright © Mometrix Media. You have been licensed one copy of this document for personal use only. Any other reproduction or redistribution is strictly prohibited. All rights reserved.
This content is provided for test preparation purposes only and does not imply an endorsement by Mometrix of any particular political, scientific, or religious point of view.